The First Book of

Modem Communications

D1608399

Jack Nimersheim

SAMS

A Division of Macmillan Computer Publishing
11711 North College, Carmel, Indiana 46032 USA

For Ralph Roberts, a fellow writer and on-line friend whom I've never met face-to-face. Maybe we will some day. Maybe we won't. Not that this matters; it's the friendship that counts.

Publisher
Richard K. Swadley

Acquisitions and Development Editor
Charlie Dresser

Technical Editor
Judy Getts Heim

Manuscript Editor
Judy J. Brunetti

Cover Artist
Held & Diedrich Design

Designer
Scott Cook

Indexer
Susan VandeWalle

Production Team
Claudia Bell
Brad Chinn
Martin Coleman
Sandy Grieshop
Denny Hager
Tami Hughes
Sarah Leatherman
Cindy L. Phipps
Dennis Sheehan
Lisa Wilson

Contents

v

vi

vii

Introduction

If I may borrow a memorable phrase from a speech once delivered by a great man: "I have a dream." It's a dream in which all the information, knowledge, and wisdom of the world is easily available to anyone, anywhere, at any time of the night or day. Does this make me some kind of pie-in-the-sky visionary who can't handle reality, and therefore must spend his days setting unattainable, utopian goals for himself and the rest of humanity?

Hardly. You see, my dream is not that far-fetched. In fact, it's already beginning to come true.

Get ready to take a trip around the world. Really. Teaching you how to traverse the globe is what this book is all about. Best of all, you can make this journey without taking a single step outside your own home. All you need to begin your amazing adventure is a personal computer, a modem, a telephone line, and a little bit of knowledge.

With this book, we will delve into the wonderful world of modem communications. In the process, you'll learn what a modem is, how it works, and some of the amazing things it allows you to accomplish. Don't panic. We won't get overly technical. I promise. My goal in this book is not to turn you into an electronic wizard. You're here to learn, to experiment, to attempt a few hands-on exercises and, I fervently hope, to have a little fun along the way.

I love firing up my PC and modem to get in touch with the world. Over the past few years, I used my modem to correspond with people from all over the world. In the process, I developed hundreds of friendships in North America, and even a few among the on-line enthusiasts on the European continent.

Don't misunderstand, however. The potential uses of a modem go far beyond establishing on-line friendships. There are dozens of ways to use a modem, and we'll take a look at all of them. Exploring the electronic world of modem communications is much like working your way through the pile of presents found under your tree on Christmas morning. You open them one at a time, and each one only increases your joy and intensifies your excitement. So, get ready to plug in a few power cords, hook up a few cables, turn a few pages, and begin learning. After you've learned enough, you'll be ready to share my dream. I'm certain of that.

Trademark Acknowledgments

All terms mentioned in this book that are known to be trademarks or service marks are listed below. In addition, terms suspected of being trademarks or service marks have been appropriately capitalized. SAMS cannot attest to the accuracy of this information. Use of a term in this book should not be regarded as affecting the validity of any trademark or service mark.

Access Plus, AT&T, AT&T Mail, and UNIX are registered trademarks of American Telephone & Telegraph Company.

Apple Macintosh and Macintosh are registered trademarks of Apple Computer, Inc.

Aterm is a registered trademark of Dynamic Microprocessor Associates, Inc.

Bell is a registered trademark of American Telephone & Telegraph Company.

BIX and Byte Information Exchange are registered trademarks of McGraw-Hill Information Services.

BLAST is a registered trademark of Communications Research Group.

BRS is a registered trademark of BRS Information Technologies.

Carbon Copy Plus is a registered trademark of Meridian Technology, Inc.

Close-Up is a registered trademark of Norton Lambert Corporation.

CompuServe, CompuServe Mail, COMPUSERVE B+, and EasyPlex are registered trademarks of CompuServe Information Services, an H & R Block Company.

CrossTalk, CrossTalk XVI, CrossTalk Mk.4, and CrossTalk Communicator are registered trademarks of Digital Communications Associates, Inc.

DELPHI is a registered trademark of General Videotex Corp.

DeskMate is a registered trademark of Tandy Corporation.

DESQview Compatible is a registered trademark of Quarterdeck Office Systems.

DIALOG is a registered trademark of Dialog Information Services, Inc.

Dow Jones News/Retrieval and The Wall Street Journal are registered trademarks of Dow Jones & Company, Inc.

x

DynaComm Asynchronous Edition is a registered trademark of Future Soft Engineering, Inc.

EasyLink is a service mark of The Western Union Telegraph Company.

EasyNet is a registered trademark of Telebase Systems, Inc.

Fax Dispatch is a registered trademark of MCI Mail.

Framework XE is a registered trademark of Ashton-Tate.

GEnie is a registered trademark of General Electric Company, U.S.A.

GeoWorks Ensemble is a registered trademark of GeoWorks.

Hayes AT, Hayes 2400 Smartmodem, and SmartCom Exec are registered trademarks of Hayes Microcomputer Products, Inc.

HyperAccess/5 is a registered trademark of Hilgrave, Inc.

IBM PS 2, IBM PC XT, and IBM 3101 are registered trademarks of International Business Machines Corporation.

KERMIT is a trademark of Henson Associates.

Lexis is a registered trademark of Mead Data Central.

Lotus 1-2-3, Lotus Symphony, and Lotus Express are registered trademarks of Lotus Development Corporation.

Mirror III is a registered trademark of SoftKlone.

MailFax is a registered trademark of AT&T Mail.

MCI Mail is a service mark of MCI Communications Corporation.

Microphone II is a registered trademark of Software Ventures Corporation.

MS-DOS, XENIX, and Microsoft Works are registered trademarks of Microsoft Corporation.

Nexis is a registered trademark of Mead Data Central.

Norton Anti-Virus is a registered trademark of Symantec Corporation.

PageMaker is a registered trademark of Aldus Corporation.

PC Anywhere IV is a registered trademark of Dynamic Microprocessor Associates, Inc.

PC Tools is a registered trademark of Central Point Software.

PC-File is a registered trademark of Buttonware, Inc.

PC-First Choice is a registered trademark of Spinnaker Software Corp.

PC-Talk is a registered trademark of Headlands Communications Corp.

PFS: First Choice is a registered trademark of Spinnaker Software Corporation.

PostScript is a registered trademark of Adobe Systems Incorporated.

PROCOMM PLUS is a registered trademark of Datastorm Technologies, Inc.

xi

Prodigy is a registered trademark of Prodigy Services Company.

Professional YAM is a registered trademark of Omen Technology, Inc.

QModem is a registered trademark of The Forbin Project, Inc.

Remote 2, R2Call, and R2Host are registered trademarks of Digital Communications Association, Inc.

Relay Gold is a registered trademark of Microcom, Inc.

Rolodex is a registered trademark of Rolodex Corporation.

SideKick 2.0 is a registered trademark of Borland International.

Sprint and SprintNet are registered trademarks of Borland International, Inc.

TAPCIS is a registered trademark of Software Group, Inc.

Toshiba T3100SX Laptop is a registered trademark of Toshiba America, Inc.

Tymnet is a registered trademark of Tymshare, Inc.

U.S. Naval Institute Military Database is a registered trademark of the United States Naval Institute.

VU/Text is a registered trademark of VU/Text Information Services, Inc.

WinComm is a registered trademark of Synappsys.

Windows is a trademark of Microsoft Corporation.

Wyse is a registered trademark of Wyse Technology, Inc.

Demystifying Modem Communications

In This Chapter

- ► *What a modem is*
- ► *How a modem works*
- ► *What a modem allows you to do*

Connecting a modem to your PC and using it to communicate with another computer for the first time can be intimidating and mysterious. Myths and misconceptions have sprouted up around modem communications like weeds around a fence post. In this chapter, we'll attempt to demystify modem communications. Along the way, we'll also attempt to debunk some of the myths and clear up many of the misconceptions surrounding the "hows" and "whys" of this particular PC application.

What Is a Modem?

A modem is your gateway to the world. Though magnanimous, that statement is not an exaggeration.

Let's face it, the personal computer is arguably the most impressive invention to emerge in the late 20th century. Few productivity tools match the potential power of a PC. Running the appropriate software, a PC can process words and crunch numbers "'til the cows come home," as the old saying goes. For many types of activities, however, even a personal computer needs help—the kind of help that requires your PC to expand its horizons beyond the four walls of your home or office.

Simply stated, a modem is a piece of equipment (called *hardware*) that is added to your PC. In this respect, a modem is not that different from any other kind of PC hardware (such as a mouse or printer). For instance, a printer enhances your PC operations by making it possible for you to produce copies of the work that you create with your PC by using a wide variety of software programs. Comparably, a modem connected to your computer will allow you to accomplish things you never could before.

The main reason for buying a modem is to allow you to connect your PC with other computers over standard telephone lines. The primary function of a modem is really that simple. As is often true when discussing PC hardware, however, describing what a modem does (i.e., how it goes about completing its assigned task) requires a more detailed explanation.

How Modems Work

So, what does a modem do? A familiar metaphor may help answer this question.

Think of a modem as resembling an AC/DC adapter, like those used with small electronic devices such as cassette recorders or cordless telephones. The primary function of these adapters is to convert the *alternating current* (AC) delivered by a standard wall outlet into the amount and type of *direct current* (DC) a given device requires to run properly. A modem works in much the same way. However, instead of modifying electrical power, it converts the *digital signals* generated internally by your PC into *analog tones*, which are then transmitted across standard telephone lines.

Hmmm...That's certainly an impressive clump of computerese, isn't it? Maybe a less technical approach is needed.

The Computer vs. the Real World

Before you jump all over me, I confess: The heading above is designed to resemble a tabloid headline (i.e., it contains a certain element of sensationalism). I understand as well as you do that computers are part of the "real world." When you think about it though, computers operate so differently from most other tools we rely on in our daily work that they do, at times, seem to have a certain surreal quality about them.

As a rule, events in our world progress smoothly from one moment to the next. If you pick up your foot to begin walking, for example, you won't find it suddenly sitting on the ground slightly in front of its previous location unless you consciously put it there. Stated another way, we live in an analog world, where events occur along a relatively predictable continuum. (I trust you'll permit me the luxury of ignoring the implications of quantum physics in this admittedly cursory explanation.) Now, compare this with what happens inside a typical PC.

That personal computer sitting on your desk is actually an intricate machine containing thousands of tiny electrical switches. (And I do mean tiny—too small to see with the naked eye.) Furthermore, much like a typical light switch, each of the electronic switches inside your PC can be set to one of two discrete positions: off or on. By "discrete" I mean there is no in-between position. In fact, there's not even a smooth transition between the two. In one instant, a switch is off. In the next, it's on.

Symbolically, we represent the current state of a given switch within a PC with one of two numerical digits (0 or 1) corresponding to off or on, respectively. For this reason, we commonly refer to a computer as being a digital device.

3

Modem Magic

If computers and telephones spoke the same "language," you would not even need a modem to connect them together. Unfortunately, this isn't the case. As explained in the previous section, virtually everything that happens inside your PC is accomplished electronically, using digital switches set to either an *off* or *on* position. A telephone, on the other hand, is an analog device, meaning it relies on continuous sound waves to function properly. (That's why the transmission of voice is successful during a telephone conversation.) The sad truth is, digital and analog devices don't get along very well with one another.

A modem functions much like an interpreter at the United Nations General Assembly. It translates information from one language to another during an on-line session (in this case, digital signals to analog tones, and vice versa), as illustrated in Figure 1.1.

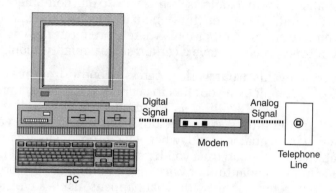

Figure 1.1 A modem converts the digital signals from your PC into analog tones compatible with the telephone system, and vice versa, during an on-line session.

4

In fact, the word modem is a contraction of *mod*ulate/*dem*odulate, technical terms used to describe how a modem works. During a communications session, a modem performs the following two essential operations:

1. When you are transmitting information, a modem converts (or modulates) the digital signals coming from your PC into signals compatible with today's analog telephone systems.
2. When you are receiving information, that same modem converts (or demodulates) the analog signals coming over the phone line from the remote computer back into the digital format required by your PC.

The precise procedures a modem follows to work its digital/analog magic are highly technical and extremely complicated. Luckily, these procedures are largely immaterial when it comes to understanding what a modem can accomplish and how to use it properly.

Suffice it to say, modems work. They work because they reliably perform the two steps previously described. So, what are the practical advantages of using a modem to call up another computer and access it from your PC? In other words, just what can you do once such a connection is made?

▶ **Note:** I don't mean to imply that learning everything there is to know about telecommunications is a waste of time. In truth, the technical side of how modems work is fascinating. If you are interested, there are several books available that delve deeply into this topic. My goal in this particular book, however, is to provide a general introduction to telecommunications, along with some pragmatic advice and information on how to use a modem, once you own one. Consequently, I'll leave the more advanced discussions to the more advanced books.

The World at Your Fingertips

Let me reiterate a statement made earlier: A modem is your gateway to the world. With a modem and the right communications software—a topic we'll be discussing in Chapter 3—it's easy to connect your PC to a computer in Atlanta or Athens, Boston or Bangkok, Hong Kong or the house next door. (As is true when placing a regular telephone call, however, some connections in this list are more expensive to make than others, a point you should remember if you don't want to end up placing your calls from the poorhouse. We'll examine the financial considerations associated with using a modem throughout this book.)

Once you know how to use a modem to link up your PC with another computer, the list of activities you can perform over such a connection is almost as diverse—and, in some cases, as exotic—as the various locations you can call. To simplify matters, let's divide this list into six categories.

1. Electronic messaging
2. Real-time conferences
3. File transfers
4. Research
5. Electronic transactions
6. Information gathering

5

Electronic Messaging

The most popular use for modem communications is currently *electronic messaging*. Estimates on the number of individuals who regularly rely on electronic messaging for at least some of their correspondence range anywhere from 8 to 15 million people. Electronic messaging is like the U.S. Postal Service—they are both *time-shifted* activities. That is, you forward an electronic message (a letter) to someone else and, if appropriate, they respond. This response, however, inevitably takes some time. The primary advantages that electronic messaging possesses over the traditional mail system are twofold: speed and convenience.

Despite the constant barrage of sarcasm it endures, you have to admire our maligned U.S. Postal Service. Every day, this nation's mail carriers deliver several billion pieces of mail reliably and in relatively short order. Moving physical items across vast distances, however, requires time. Even under the best of circumstances, it's not unreasonable to expect several days to pass before a letter mailed from New York finally makes its way to a California address.

By contrast, electronic messages can be passed back and forth (if not instantaneously) in a matter of seconds, regardless of the distances involved. If the intended recipient of a given message is alerted to its arrival, he or she can dispatch a response with comparable speed.

Electronic messaging is also convenient, especially for those on the receiving end. Once you subscribe to an electronic mail service, you no longer have to wait for days for the mail carrier to deliver an important message. Rather, you can check on its status as your schedule permits by simply dialing the appropriate phone number and seeing whether any mail has been forwarded to your electronic address.

In short, electronic messaging promises to revolutionize how we communicate with one another. To share in the advantages associated with this new communications medium, however, you need to get a modem and some kind of communications software up and running on your PC. Don't worry. We'll begin outlining the steps involved in accomplishing this shortly. For now, we still have a few more modem-related activities to look at.

Real-Time Conferences

If electronic messaging resembles traditional mail service, then *real-time conferencing* is similar to using a multiline telephone to initiate a conference call—or, perhaps even more apropos, a computerized variation of the CB craze that swept the country a few years back. During real-time conferencing several callers chat with one another by typing in comments at their keyboards. Pressing the Enter key causes what you have typed to display on the screens of everyone else involved in the current conference.

Almost all commercial on-line information services (CompuServe, GEnie, DELPHI, Prodigy, and the like) support on-line conferencing. (We'll profile several of the more popular commercial services, including the ones listed here, in Chapter 7.) Every Thursday night, for example, I make it a point to visit the Writers' Conference on DELPHI, where established and would-be writers get together to discuss various aspects of what it takes to make it as a writer. Some weeks are devoted to structured discussions. More common, however, are informal gatherings, where we all get together and let the conversation wander. With a dozen or more people participating in this conference on any given Thursday night, something of interest almost always comes up. Like most conference groups, ours evolved informally over time, as I and several of my fellow DELPHI users realized that we shared a common interest: writing with one another.

7

File Transfers

One of the most practical uses for a modem is to transfer files between two computers. To some extent, this is what happens when you send someone an electronic message. However, the information you transfer over a modem link isn't limited to simple correspondence. Even more useful is the ability to transmit actual data files across phone lines.

For example, suppose a potential investor in a distant city told you that he wanted to see the business plan you put together for a new enterprise—and, he wanted to see it quickly. Providing the two of you owned the same application programs (word processor, spreadsheet, graphics program, etc.), you could establish a modem connection and transmit the actual data files used to create this plan for his review. Voilà! Instant communications and, quite possibly, venture capital.

Another benefit associated with transferring files over a modem connection is that it allows you to exchange text files between otherwise incompatible systems. It's a sad fact of PC life, but different types of personal computers use different file and disk formats to store their data files. It's virtually impossible, therefore, to use a file created with an Apple Macintosh, for example, on an IBM-compatible PC—at least, not without first going through all kinds of electronic gymnastics to translate the file from one system's disk format to the other's. Because the IBM automatically stores data coming across a phone line in its own disk format, transferring the same file over a modem link eliminates this problem.

Research

How would you like to be able to access a wealth of information, literally at the touch of a button—or, in this case, keyboard? That's a pretty good description of what *on-line research* is all about.

If you need a fact or figure, whether it be of a general or specialized nature, chances are you'll find it in an on-line database. There are many areas of interest covered, in one form or another, on a number of public and private on-line services such as news services like the Associated Press and Reuters, financial information from sources as diverse as the New York Stock Exchange and Dow/Jones, historical records, business news, economic studies, medical research, and statistics galore. Additionally, commercial services such as CompuServe and GEnie offer easy access to one or more on-line encyclopedias that are used to research more general projects like homework assignments and term papers.

I should warn you, however, that, as a rule, research databases carry fairly steep access charges for the time you spend on-line using them. The rate per minute for using a specialized research database is generally higher than that charged by the more popular commercial services such as CompuServe and GEnie. Some commercial services also levy an additional surcharge, on top of their regular rates, for any time you spend accessing a dedicated research database such as an on-line encyclopedia or wire service.

Electronic Transactions

I have a vague memory from my youth of reading a science fiction story about a man who lived his entire life in a single room. The main premise behind this fascinating story (the name and author have been wiped from my mind's slate by the intervening years) was that technology had become so advanced that everything you would ever need could either be bought or simulated with a powerful "thinking machine," which bore a close resemblance to a modern computer. The protagonist in this story never left the safety of his bountiful yet artificial environment; nor did he ever need to. Although our own society is not yet this machine-dependent—and, in truth, I hope it never becomes so—we're definitely beginning to rely more and more on gadgets and gizmos to simplify our lives.

It's now possible, for example, to order a wide variety of goods and services on-line through either dedicated computer stores or commercial services. Financial transactions such as the buying and selling of stocks, electronic banking, and even automating your monthly check-writing activities can be initiated from the comfort of your own home, using a PC and modem.

Will there come a time when we'll be able to fulfill all our needs without ever once stepping out the front door, like the story of my youth suggests? As stated earlier, I certainly hope not. Used wisely, however, the ability to shop at home can be a welcome convenience in these modern times when, more often than not, time is a rare commodity, indeed.

Information Gathering

Information gathering is a refined type of research. I differentiate between the two here because what I call *information gathering* is much more than simply going on-line to investigate an explicit subject for a specific project or activity.

Imagine you could subscribe to a newspaper that covered only the stories that were important to *you*. Wouldn't it be nice to go to your door each morning and find a daily paper devoted exclusively to only those topics? The "My Daily News," so to speak.

Several on-line services now allow you to specify search parameters for news stories, financial coverage, and the like. Any stories relating to the topics you find interesting are automatically flagged for your review the next time you call in. What we're talking about here is exactly the kind of personalized, communications newspaper described in the previous paragraph—without the paper. On-line services are the perfect vehicle for the ultimate attainment of this ideal information-gathering process.

9

> **Note:** As stated at the beginning of this section, many people do not differentiate between research and information gathering. In my mind, however, research is a one-shot, project-oriented effort, such as using an on-line database to look up information to use in a specific report, assignment, or project. Simply stated, on-line research is an electronic extension of more traditional research methods. By contrast, I define information gathering as an on-going activity—unique to the computer age when even such a mundane activity like reading the newspaper becomes so personalized that the electronic newspaper transmitted over my modem to my PC reads completely different from the one delivered to my next door neighbor. In truth, this conflict of opinion doesn't bother me. After all, even experts can agree to disagree.

10

Are you beginning to see the potential advantages associated with modem communications? Are you also beginning to realize there's nothing mysterious or mythical about how modem communications work? We're talking about a very real phenomenon here—one you can begin experiencing as soon as you learn some very basic (and, honestly, not overly complicated) procedures. In the next chapter, we'll "get our feet wet" as we begin looking at the various steps involved in hooking up a modem to your PC and using that modem to communicate with other computers. We'll also look at the unique language of modem communications—or "ModemSpeak," as I like to call it.

What You Have Learned

▶ A modem is a piece of computer hardware that allows you to use your PC to connect with other computers over standard telephone lines.

▶ The primary function of a modem is to convert the digital signals generated by your computer into analog tones, which are then transmitted across telephone lines to a second computer. The same modem converts incoming analog tones from the other computer into the digital signals required by your PC.

► You can use a modem to call many different types of computers and initiate many different types of on-line activities. Among the more popular of these are electronic messaging, real-time conferencing, file transfers, research, electronic transactions, and information gathering.

11

Chapter 2

Understanding "ModemSpeak"

In This Chapter

▶ *The language of modem communications*
▶ *How a PC handles information during a modem connection*
▶ *How modems use parameters and protocols to communicate successfully with one another*

As any experienced traveler knows, visiting a foreign country is much more enjoyable if you possess at least a working knowledge of its native language. Rather than constantly having to strain your brain to comprehend what's going on around you, this allows you to sit back, relax, and enjoy the scenery. Reading a computer book is a lot like that. If you spend all your time trying to comprehend the words printed on the page, you'll never get around to understanding the more important message behind them.

In this chapter we'll look at the often exotic language of modem communications, or what I call *ModemSpeak*. This is more than just a "Berlitz Course on Modems," however. The terms introduced here also serve as a springboard for discussing several concepts critical to understanding how modems work. This knowledge, in turn, will prove useful throughout the rest of this book, as we delve more deeply into the specific steps involved in using your modem to expand the horizons of your PC activities.

Tele-What?

Some of you may be wondering why I've shied away from using the more common term, *telecommunications*, to describe what this book is all about. Specifically, the *tele* prefix is attached to so many objects and operations associated with using a modem that, in the end, it confuses rather than clarifies.

There's telecommunications, telecommuting, telecomputing, tele-conferencing, teleservices, and…well, you get the picture. To "tele" you the truth, even I get befuddled from time to time. Let's begin at the beginning, therefore, and see if we can muddle our way through this morass of teleterms, so to speak.

Telecommunications

14

Have you been looking for a single sentence that explains what telecommunications is? If so, you're in luck. I happen to have one. To wit: "Telecommunications is the process of using your PC, a modem, and special software to communicate with other computers over standard telephone lines." Get it? *Tele*phone *communications* between two computers. Telecommunications. That's really all there is to it.

In essence, telecommunications is a catch-all phrase that encom-passes all of the various activities for which a modem is used. Whenever the word telecommunications appears in this book, therefore, that's exactly how I'll be using it—interchangeably with what I feel to be a more precise term, *modem communications*.

Telecommuting

In his 1981 book, *The Electronic Cottage*, author Joseph Deken describes a world in which a large portion of the work force no longer faces the daily grind of traveling back and forth to their corporate offices. Rather, these people work at home, using a personal computer and a modem whenever they need to interact with their fellow employees or, even more common, access a central source of information.

This was pretty heavy stuff way back in 1981. After all, when Deken's book was first published, IBM had not yet officially introduced its now-legendary PC/XT—a system that many experts contend ultimately established the personal computer as a legitimate business tool. How times change....

Today, millions of people work exactly as Deken described. They *telecommute* using their personal computer, a modem, and standard telephone lines to perform a wide range of tasks that once required commuting on a daily basis to a centralized work place.

Telecomputing

A modem allows your PC to do much more than merely make contact with other computers. Using the right software, you can actually take control of a distant computer, tell it what to do, and make it run as if it were sitting on a desk right in front of you, connected directly to your own keyboard and monitor. The teleterm for this process is *telecomputing* (i.e., operating a computer at a remote site over standard telephone lines).

15

Teleconferencing

Teleconferencing is applied to activities that take place both in and out of the realm of personal computers. (Although, like so many other activities, computers coordinate virtually all teleconferencing that goes on in the world today.) Businesses use teleconferencing to hold meetings where several people in several different locations share an audio and visual hookup, allowing all of them to assemble in the same place at the same time.

In the PC world, teleconferencing refers specifically to when two or more people are communicating with one another in *real time* over a modem connection. As mentioned in the previous chapter, most commercial on-line services now sponsor organized teleconferencing sessions, where people all over the world can get together on a regular basis and discuss their shared interests. (We'll discuss teleconferencing in greater detail in Chapter 6.)

Teleservices

Teleservices comprise a number of activities that reportedly will be supported by the *Integrated Services Digital Network* (ISDN), a proposed transition from reliance on our current analog phone systems to a complete digitization of the world's telecommunications. (Fiberoptic technology is the first, faltering step down the road toward this goal.) Even some of the most optimistic experts agree that it will be at least 10 to 15 years before the dream of ISDN becomes a reality. More pragmatic predictions place the realization of this digital dream even further into the future. If and when ISDN becomes a reality, the list of teleservices that you should be able to access over this single, global communications network, using a single phone line, will include:

▶ Telephone conversations
▶ Teletex (an electronic descendent of the old telex systems)
▶ Facsimile services
▶ Videotex (graphic images transmitted across ISDN)
▶ Telex (nonmodem text communications)
▶ Electronic mail delivery

All this may sound like the stuff of which science fiction is made, but 10 years is not really a long time in today's world. After all, it was only slightly over a decade ago that the first personal computers started appearing on the market.

The Basic "B" Words

We'll begin by examining what I like to refer to as the *B words* (several terms used to describe how, and how quickly, data is exchanged between two computers during an on-line session).

Specifically, these words include:

▶ *Bit.* A contraction for *binary digit*, a bit is the smallest unit of information a computer is capable of handling.
▶ *Byte.* A grouping of bits.
▶ *Block.* An organized set of bits or bytes.

- ▶ *Bit Rate.* A measurement of how quickly data is transferred between two computers.
- ▶ *Baud.* The number of signal transitions that occur within a phone line each second.

Now that we have these rudimentary definitions to work with, let's see how the B words influence your modem communications. We'll begin with the bit, the smallest unit of information a computer is capable of handling.

Bits

Within your PC, a *bit* corresponds to the current state (i.e., off or on) of each of the literally tens of thousands of electronic switches, or memory addresses, it contains. As pointed out in the previous chapter, the state of a specific memory address within your PC is symbolically represented by the number 0 or 1 (off or on, respectively), a technique called *binary notation*.

Think of this as resembling Morse Code—a different, but possibly more familiar, communications technique based on a form of binary notation. In Morse Code, dots and dashes represent single bits of information, a process that makes them analogous to the zeros and ones common to computer jargon.

However, how much *real* information can a single bit (or, alternately, a dot or dash) convey? Not much. To designate anything other than the difference between two states or items—off/on, dot/dash—it's necessary to combine several bits into a larger unit of information called a *byte*.

Bytes

By organizing bits into bytes and then assigning unique byte patterns to specific codes, your computer can use the on/off status of its individual memory addresses—those symbolic zeros and ones mentioned earlier—to represent letters, numbers, and other truly useful information. Once again, this is similar to how Morse Code utilizes dots and dashes.

Most people would recognize *dot-dot-dot dash-dash-dash dot-dot-dot* (· · · − − − · · ·) as the Morse Code sequence for SOS, an international distress signal. In an emergency, therefore, someone familiar with this

17

pattern can use merely nine bits of data—three dots, followed by three dashes, followed by three more dots—to communicate (if you'll pardon the pun) quite a bit of very critical information. Specifically, the implied message: "I'm in trouble and need help." Computers utilize bytes in a similar manner. For example, *ASCII*, one popular form of binary notation we'll discuss shortly, uses the 7-bit byte 1000001 to represent an uppercase A.

In this way, binary notation allows your computer to convey complex information (such as a complete work) by simply generating the appropriate sequence of bytes. Even recognizing the incredible speeds at which computers operate, however, sending a long message over a telephone line one byte (and, therefore, one character) at a time is an extremely slow process. The obvious way around this problem is to combine individual bytes into even larger units. In turn, this leads directly to a discussion of the third B word listed earlier, the block.

18 *Blocks*

During most sessions of modem communications, data is transmitted and received in *blocks*, a much more efficient method than if the same information passed back and forth one single bit or byte at a time. For one thing, the actual process of organizing bits into bytes, and then combining those bytes into blocks, is all accomplished internally—that is, within the *random access memory* (RAM) installed in your PC. Since RAM is by far the fastest component of any computer, this happens much more quickly than if individual bits of data were processed elsewhere. Second, and perhaps more important, once a block exists, it is transferred automatically to a special buffer (another B word), which resembles an electronic "holding cell" for data.

The actual transfer of data to another computer does not occur until this buffer is relatively full (i.e., until several blocks are prepared for transmission using the steps outlined above). Taken together, these steps (all of which are initiated and coordinated by a special kind of software called a *communications program*) allow for the rapid exchange of information between two computers, even using today's outdated and noise-riddled phone lines.

How rapid? Well, calculating this gets a little tricky and requires a discussion of still another term introduced earlier, bit rate.

Bit Rate

As a general rule, *bit rate* (which, as you'll recall, we defined as the measurement of how quickly data transfers between two computers) is expressed in *bits-per-second* (bps). Ostensibly, bit rate means exactly what you might expect (i.e., the number of bits moving through a phone line at any given time). How much real information this data represents, however, depends on several factors.

To begin with, remember that your PC requires more than a single bit to depict an actual letter, number, or other piece of useful information. For example, as previously explained, the ASCII notation for an uppercase A (1000001) requires seven bits. In the best of all possible worlds, therefore, an on-line connection configured to use ASCII code and a bit rate of 2400 bps permits a little over 342 characters—2400 bps divided by 7-bits-per-character—to be exchanged each second.

Modem communications, however, do not take place in the best of all possible worlds. In fact, the actual amount of information flowing through a phone line during a 2400-bps session may be considerably less, since it also is influenced by several other technical aspects of telecommunications that we'll examine in the pages ahead. For right now, we'll wrap up our current discussion by looking at the fifth and final B word, baud.

19

Baud

Baud is perhaps the most misused term in the unique lexicon of modem communications. Many people think of baud as being analogous to bit rate or bps. It isn't.

Technically, a baud has nothing to do with your computer or modem. Rather, it is strictly a function of the phone line over which a modem connection is established. As I've already pointed out several times, most telephone lines today still depend on analog transmission methods. As I've also explained previously, however, a computer is a digital device (i.e., it uses the discrete off/on state of its electronic switches to convey information). Consequently, an analog device (such as a telephone) must employ some technological sleight-of-hand if it is to successfully transmit the "pure" digital signals coming from your personal computer.

The solution to this problem is called a *baud*. Technically, a baud (named after the French communications pioneer, Baudot) is any change in the frequency, voltage level, or phase angle within a tradi-tional, analog communications channel such as a standard phone line. A modem's primary job is to convert the digital signals coming from your PC into one of these analog phenomena.

During a given telecommunications session, for example, your modem may translate any zeros (off states) it receives into one fre-quency. Conversely, on states (our symbolic ones) are converted into a second, yet different, frequency. Only after this conversion takes place is your modem able to transmit digital data through the phone lines as individual baud or frequency changes. (A modem at the other end of the connection performs this same function in reverse, converting the analog frequencies it receives back into digital signals, which are then used by the computer to which it is attached.)

The biggest problem with this arrangement is that there's a practical limit to the number of baud a traditional, analog telephone line can reliably handle each second (defined as its *maximum baud rate*). For a number of technical reasons, this limit is 2400 baud, or 2400 changes in frequency per second.

If you're already familiar with how modems work, however, you're probably aware that today's modems support transmission speeds much higher than this—4800 bps, 9600 bps, and more. Although the two terms are often used interchangeably, therefore, the baud and bit rate of a given on-line session are not always identical to one another, a fact pointed out at the beginning of this admittedly convoluted explanation.

Minding Your "P's and Q's"

In truth, two modems communicate over a telephone line in much the same way two people would: they pass information back and forth between one another. That is, one modem *says* something into one end of a phone connection, and a second modem on the other end of this connection *hears* that message, which it then converts into the digital signals required by your PC.

Like we communicate with words, modems communicate with bits, bytes, and blocks of data. These items comprise the language of telecommunications. As two people must share a common language to talk on a telephone, however, the two modems involved in an on-line session must "speak the same language" before they can carry on a successful conversation.

So, how do you accomplish this? There are, after all, no Berlitz courses available for use with a modem—at least, none that I'm aware of. Fortunately, however, most communications programs allow you to use special settings, called *communications parameters*, to basically allow communicating in the same "language."

Parameters

Your modem relies on communications parameters to determine how it exchanges information with another modem during an on-line session. These parameters consist of several settings you specify using a communications program and include, among other things, baud rate (or, more precisely, bps), data bits, stop bits, and parity.

Baud rate

In the previous section, it was stated that one of the B words of ModemSpeak (baud) was probably the most misused term in telecommunications. Well, guess what? It's used incorrectly here. Technically, this setting should be identified as bps (i.e., the number of bits that can ideally be transmitted or received by each modem each second). However, since they call it *baud rate*, we'll call it baud rate.

> ▶ **Note:** This brings up an interesting problem regularly confronted by technical writers. Specifically, should we stand our journalistic ground and insist on using terminology that is technically correct, or stick with the familiar expressions that have filtered down into the popular vocabulary? That's a tough question. I understand that bps is the most technically correct term, however, the vast majority of communications programs currently on the market still employ baud rate to identify the setting used when selecting a transmission speed for your modem. In this case, at least, it strikes me that insisting on referring to this value as bps only serves to confuse the reader that consistently sees baud in his or her communications program.

21

Today's modems support a wide range of baud settings, ranging from 100 to figures higher than 100,000. The two most common settings for the majority of telecommunications activities, however, are 1200 and 2400, with 9600 slowly but surely gaining in popularity. One thing to keep in mind is that the advertised speed of a modem is generally the fastest speed at which that modem can communicate. A 2400-baud modem, for example, also supports 1200-, 300-, and even 100-baud connections.

Many modems also include a feature called *Auto Detect*, which determines the baud rate at which another modem is operating and adjusts itself accordingly. This feature can be invaluable if you are uncertain of the proper baud setting the first time you call a remote system.

Data Bits and Stop Bits

Data bits and stop bits define how your modem organizes and transmits data during an on-line session (i.e., how individual bits organize into larger chunks of information). You will recall that a bit is the smallest piece of data that your PC can process. Remember, though, that it takes more than one bit to convert this raw data (the individual on and off switch settings) into useful information, where the data- and stop-bits settings come into play.

The *data-bit* setting used during a given on-line session specifies the number of individual bits that are used to indicate a single character. This is commonly referred to as the length of a data word. Most commercial programs allow you to set this value to either 7 or 8.

When computers communicate in 7-bit data words, they are limited to sending each other text such as letters, numbers, and the more common punctuation marks. Increasing the word length to 8 bits allows binary data—for example, files containing so-called high-bit characters such as executable (COM and EXE) files and data files created by many application programs—to be transferred over a modem. Many mainframe computers are limited to communicating in 7-bit data words. Within the PC world, however, the use of 8-bit data words prevails. A good rule of thumb, therefore, is to configure your communications software for 7-bit data word transmissions whenever you're dialing an on-line service that uses a mainframe computer, such as CompuServe. Conversely, you should specify an 8-bit setting for PC-to-PC connections, as would be the case when calling a local bulletin board.

I know I'm starting to sound like a broken record, but the critical point is to use the same data-bit setting on both systems involved in an on-line session.

Stop bits are used to indicate the end of a character comprised of multiple data bits. They tell the modem on the receiving end: "This is the end of the current character bit sequence. Go ahead and display this character to the computer screen." (Or, alternately, copy it to a disk file.) The most common stop-bits settings are 1 and 2. (And, yes, the stop-bits setting must be the same on both systems.)

Parity

As reliable as today's phone systems may be, they aren't perfect. Originally designed to handle the continuous sound waves that make up the human voice, they require all kinds of electronic juggling to transmit the discrete, on/off signals generated by a digital device such as your PC. This, you may recall, is the primary reason you must use a modem to telecommunicate. A drop in the quality of a telephone connection caused by hisses, echoes, and static bursts, commonly referred to as *line noise*, can wreak havoc on your computer's attempts to converse successfully with another computer.

One way to avoid the types of errors that can result from line noise is to have your communications software attach a *parity bit* to each character it sends, which the software on the other end of the connection then uses to verify that the bit pattern of the character it receives matches what was transmitted. Today's modems rely on one of the following three parity settings:

- ▶ Odd
- ▶ Even
- ▶ None

With error checking enabled, the communications software uses an extra bit to make the individual bits in a character correspond to the specified parity.

For example, suppose that you transmit a capital C in the 7-bit ASCII format mentioned earlier, using *Even parity*. The ASCII code for C is 1000011. The sum of its individual bits, therefore, would be the odd number 3.

To achieve Even parity, your software would add an extra 1 to the end of this bit pattern and actually transmit 10000111. The software at the other end would also be set to Even parity and checked to see whether the bit pattern it received added up to an even number. If it did, then that character would pass on—minus, of course, the parity bit. If not, it assumed that an error occurred and would request that this character be retransmitted.

23

Conversely, if *Odd parity* was specified, a 0 parity bit would have been added to our sample C. As a result, the sum of its individual bits remained an odd number.

Selecting the Third Parity option, *None*, effectively disables data verification at the character level.

Yes, here we go again: Both computers involved in a modem connection must agree on what kind of parity to use during a given on-line session and whether or not they will use it.

Putting It All Together

Now that we've discussed each of these items, let's see how they combine into a single set of communications parameters. Suppose, for example, that you wanted to call another computer for which you had a telephone number, followed by the numbers 2400,N,8,1. As you may have guessed, this notation indicates that the system in question supports communications parameters of 2400 baud, no parity, 8 data bits, and 1 stop bit. Prior to calling that board, therefore, you would need to use the appropriate command in your communications software to specify these settings for the current session. (We'll get into how you do this with specific packages in Chapter 4.)

If you ever connect to a remote system and see an odd assortment of characters and symbols that makes no sense—what we high-tech computer types call *garbage*—the most likely culprit is a parameter mismatch. Don't panic. In many cases, changing the current settings to create a different configuration, something most communications programs allow you to do at any time during an on-line session, will solve this problem.

Protocols

Another time when it's important for modems to coordinate their activities closely is when a file is transferred between the two. During a file transfer, the two computers must agree not only on which parameters to use (baud rate, data bit settings, and parity), but also on whether or not they will verify the quality of the transmission and how they will verify it.

Suppose, for example, that you are chatting on-line with someone and send the message `Hi, Bob.` to that individual. While this greeting is transmitted, line noise from the telephone connection causes it to include superfluous characters, so that what Bob sees on his end is utter gibberish resembling, `H#,ggi*,Brero(%b`. If this should happen during a real conversation, Bob would simply type back, `Sorry, that last sentence was garbled. What did you say?`—thus, telling you a problem had occurred and allowing you to try once more to transmit the message successfully. During a file transfer, however, when interaction between your computer and the remote system is fully automated, similar error-checking procedures must be implemented automatically to guarantee that line noise does not contaminate that file's contents. Several standard file-transfer protocols evolved through the years for precisely this purpose.

Understanding how these protocols work—that is, the precise procedures a specific protocol uses to detect and, whenever appropriate, correct errors—is less important than knowing which protocol you should select for a given file-transfer operation.

25

Selecting the Proper Protocol

Many times, the protocol you select to transfer a file is determined by the remote system with which that file is exchanged. If the remote system only supports ASCII file transfers, for example, then ASCII protocol must be used. Other times, however, you may choose from different options. Several factors will determine which protocol to specify, including:

- ▶ How the transferred file is formatted, which is determined primarily by the word length of the data it contains
- ▶ Whether or not that file includes control characters (nonprinting characters which help define the information it contains)
- ▶ How large a block of data you want to exchange at a time during a file transfer
- ▶ The type of error-checking you want applied to each data block transferred between the sending and receiving computer

Perhaps the biggest factor influencing your choice of protocols is the type of file you transfer. This leads directly into a discussion of another stunning example of ModemSpeak, one that also applies to virtually all PC applications.

ASCII vs. Binary

Virtually every file you transfer is one of two primary file types:

► ASCII
► Binary

In some ways, these two terms are misleading, in that only the latter one, binary, is a true description of the file format it represents.

ASCII Protocol

Basically, an ASCII file is a file in which all the characters it contains are represented by decimal numbers, 0 through 128. (An uppercase A, for example, is represented by the decimal value 65.) Since 128 equals 2 raised to the seventh power, the maximum number of bits able to be sent or received as a byte of data during an ASCII file transfer is seven. The *ASCII protocol* is alternately (and, therefore, more correctly) referred to as a *7-bit protocol*.

Of course, since only a few bit values (128) are available during a 7-bit file transfer, the type of information you can exchange with an ASCII protocol is similarly limited. For the most part, ASCII protocol is used to transfer straight text files, which are documents whose contents are limited to upper- and lowercase letters (A through Z and a through z), numeric characters (0 through 9), punctuation marks (!,@,#, etc.), and a few formatting codes such as line feeds, carriage returns, blank spaces, and the like.

As a rule, most electronic mail services use ASCII file transfers (or some proprietary version of the same) to send and deliver messages to and from their subscribers.

Binary Files

Binary files, on the other hand, consist of 8-bit data bytes, in which each bit represents the binary digit, 0 or 1. Since 2 raised to the eighth power is 256, this effectively doubles the number of letters, numeric characters, control codes, formatting instructions, etc., that are transferred with a binary protocol. Virtually all executable programs (i.e., files ending in EXE or COM) must be transferred using some type of binary protocol.

26

So ends our introductory course on ModemSpeak. We covered a lot of territory in this chapter. Hopefully, it didn't confuse you too much. If some of the terms and concepts introduced here are still somewhat unclear, don't worry. They'll resurface and be explained further within the context of specific on-line activities in the chapters to follow. We have laid the foundation for what follows, a discussion of the tools (hardware and software) needed to begin telecommunicating.

What You Have Learned

▶ The general term *telecommunications* encompasses a wide range of activities including telecommuting, telecomputing, teleconferencing, and the like. Specifically, telecommunications is the process of using your PC, a modem, and special software to communicate with other computers over standard telephone lines.

▶ Personal computers—and, by extension, modems—organize individual pieces of information into structures called bits, bytes, and data blocks. The manner in which these items are formatted influences how they are exchanged during an on-line session.

▶ For two modems to communicate successfully with one another, they must use identical communications parameters— that is, the data exchanged between the two must be formatted and transmitted the same way by both modems. Protocols serve a similar purpose, whenever files are transferred over a modem connection.

27

What You'll Need

In This Chapter

► *The physical equipment (hardware) required to telecommunicate*

► *Choosing the right communications software*

► *How to set up a telephone line for modem communications*

► *How to use a surge-suppressor to protect your PC and modem*

Few PC activities offer the same price/prize advantages inherent in telecommunications. For a relatively small initial investment you can build an electronic doorway that leads, quite literally, to the rest of the world. How's that for a deal? In this chapter we will discuss what you need and how much (or, more correctly, how little) it will cost you to begin telecommunicating.

Easy on the Hardware Budget

The basic hardware (i.e., the actual physical components) required to telecommunicate consists of two items:

▶ a personal computer
▶ a modem

With nothing more than these two items you can begin electronically exploring the world from the comfort of your own home.

Of course, the specific kind of PC and modem you need depends largely on what types of activities you'll be performing. The options available are almost limitless. Rather than telling you what combination of PC and modem you should buy, let's take a look at some that are out there and discuss the advantages and disadvantages associated with each.

30

Picking the Right PC

Personal computers come in all shapes and sizes, yet all of them support telecommunications. How do you choose the one that's right for you? Let's break the factors down into four main categories, which I call "the critical P's for selecting a PC."

▶ Power
▶ Price
▶ Portability
▶ Popularity

PC Power

Perhaps the most surprising aspect of telecommunications is how little PC power it demands. The memory requirements of most communications software are minimal. Even if your PC has only 256K of memory, it should be able to run any one of several competent communications programs. Furthermore, because of the limitations that today's phone systems place on how quickly data is exchanged between computers, speed also becomes a moot point when choosing a PC to manage your on-line activities. A basic PC/XT unit built around a first-generation 8088 or 8086 microprocessor has more than enough power for modem connections.

If you think about it, speed and memory are two of the primary factors consumers look at when choosing the most appropriate system for almost any PC application. Therefore, if a computer you're considering can handle electronic spreadsheet, word processing, database management, or any of the other popular PC activities, then chances are it allows access to other computers. However, it must provide some way for you to connect a modem, the key component for telecommunications.

As you will see shortly, modems come in two basic models: *internal* and *external*. If you decide to purchase an external modem, make certain that your PC includes a serial port. A *serial port* is an electronic door, through which information can pass to and from your PC.

Some PCs have a serial port built into them as part of their basic system configuration. Others require that you install an *expansion card* that includes a serial port inside your unit.

The alternative to an external modem is an internal model. As their name implies, internal modems are installed in an *expansion slot* inside your PC. To accept an internal modem, therefore, a PC must either have a free expansion slot available or include a special slot designed exclusively for a modem. This last feature, a dedicated modem slot, is commonly found in laptop computers.

31

> ▶ **Note:** Chapter 4 contains more information on serial ports and expansion slots, including the specific steps involved in installing an internal/external modem in your PC.

The Price is Right

You don't really need a super-powerful PC to telecommunicate. That's good news if you're operating on a tight budget. The price of a first-generation MS-DOS computer (i.e., an IBM or compatible PC built around an 8088 or 8086 microprocessor, often called *PC/XT systems*) has dropped to ridiculously low levels over the past few years. Many reputable mail-order houses now sell PC/XT systems, complete with a graphics monitor and hard disk, for less than $500. (You'll begin to get a better idea of how much PC prices have dropped over the past decade when I tell you that I spent over $2,000 on my first IBM-compatible about 7 years ago—and that was without the hard disk.)

Of course, the more powerful and expensive your PC, the more you can to do with it. The nice thing about telecommunications is that because it demands so little in the way of system resources, it leaves a lot of potential power remaining for other activities. Having retired that initial IBM-compatible PC several years ago, I now rely on a third-generation MS-DOS system that uses the Intel 80386 microprocessor for all my PC operations. Because the 80386 chip supports multitasking (the ability to run more than one program at a time), I can work in other applications while my modem takes care of the 'droid work, without my even being aware that it's doing so.

How much you spend on a PC to coordinate your modem communications is your decision. An inexpensive system works just fine. A more expensive, state-of-the-art PC works better, especially if you use it to run other, high-end applications.

PC Portability

32

A modem and a laptop computer are natural companions. Think about it. The primary purpose of a laptop computer is to allow you to travel virtually anywhere in the world and still carry your PC power with you. The main function of a modem, as I pointed out at the beginning of this chapter, is to let you visit faraway places (electronically) without ever having to leave the comfort of your own home. Connecting a modem with a laptop provides you with the best of both possible worlds. From your home base, you can make connections to distant lands; and when you're traveling those distant lands, home is but a phone call away.

The PC Popularity Contest

At first glance, it might strike you as strange that I include popularity in my list of items that should influence your PC purchasing decisions. How well a product sells is not *always* a reliable indicator of how well it performs.

Even admitting this, however, popularity should influence your decision on which system is best for you, for one very important reason: In the PC arena, there's definitely strength in numbers. The more successful a particular type of PC is, the more diverse the selection of ancillary products available for that PC (both hardware and software) will be.

By far the most popular types of personal computers currently on the market are those that use the MS-DOS operating system, more commonly referred to as *IBM-compatible PCs*. It's estimated that over 40 million people own and use MS-DOS systems. Any manufacturer in its right mind would love to have its name on a product that appeals to even a small percentage of such a potentially lucrative market. Consequently, hardware and software alternatives are increasing for MS-DOS systems.

Allow me, therefore, to state this as diplomatically as possible: If you're in the market for a personal computer, you really should check out the MS-DOS market. Unless you have a compelling reason for purchasing a system other than one that's IBM-compatible—as would be the case, if you work for a company that exclusively uses a different PC platform—no other decision makes sense. (I should point out that I will be relying on MS-DOS hardware and software for any examples and exercises contained in this book.)

33

Modem Madness

When the time comes to choose a modem, things get a little more complicated. Next, we'll examine some of the factors you must consider when deciding which type of modem is right for you.

The "Ins" and "Outs" of Modems

As stated previously, modems come in two basic models:

- ▶ internal modems
- ▶ external modems

An internal modem is installed within your PC by inserting it into an open expansion slot. These are generally lined-up along the back of a PC's motherboard and used to hold a variety of specialized boards such as extra memory, a disk controller, your display card, and the like, as illustrated in Figure 3.1.

Motherboard   Expansion Slots   Input/Output (I/O) Ports   Microprocessor (CPU)

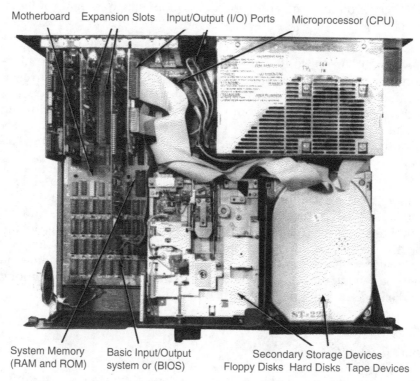

System Memory   Basic Input/Output   Secondary Storage Devices
(RAM and ROM)   system or (BIOS)   Floppy Disks Hard Disks Tape Devices

*Figure 3.1 An internal modem is installed inside your PC,
using its built-in expansion slots.*

An external modem, on the other hand, is a separate, stand-alone
piece of equipment, like the one shown in Figure 3.2. Since it does not
plug directly into the motherboard, an external modem must be
connected to your PC through a standard serial port.

Functionally, internal and external modems are virtually identical
to one another. Choosing one over the other, therefore, is pretty much
a matter of personal preference and price. In some cases, however, this
decision can also be influenced by your hardware configuration.

Based on purely economic considerations, an internal modem is
the more logical choice. Prices for 1200-baud internal modems have
dropped dramatically over the past few years, to the point where you
can now pick one up for under $100 through any number of reputable
mail-order firms. For an extra $50, you can double the speed of your
modem communications by purchasing a 2400-baud internal modem
from one of these same companies.

Figure 3.2 An external modem is connected to your PC through a serial port.

If all available expansion slots in your PC are full, then an external modem is the only option. Conversely, if all the serial ports on your system are already being used for other hardware components (like a mouse or a serial printer), then you need to use an internal modem.

⊘ **Caution:** One mandatory precaution you must take when installing an internal modem in an older computer is to make certain it doesn't overload your PC's power supply. Unlike external modems, which plug directly into a wall outlet, internal modems draw their electrical power from your system's expansion bus. Back in the seminal days of personal computers, an 85-watt power supply was enough to power all of the peripherals we pioneers of the PC revolution would be tempted to add to our systems. We proved to be a greedy bunch, however, and quickly outgrew those early predictions. Today's more powerful PCs come equipped with more robust power supplies (such as 150 to 200 watts, minimum). If you have an older system, be careful that you do not place too many demands on its power supply.

The Speed Factor

The second factor you must consider when deciding whether or not to buy a particular modem is its advertised baud rate. Baud rate measures the number of times per second that a signal varies within a modem; that is, how it changes between two states (from one frequency to another, one voltage to another, and the like—mechanisms modems use to represent digital signals over an analog phone line). A 2400-baud modem, therefore, is theoretically capable of changing states 2400 times per second. However, a single baud need not necessarily correspond to a *bit* of information (a digital 0 or 1). One communications line might need less, while another might need more. On a communications line where two baud are needed to send a single bit of information, therefore, a 2400-baud modem could achieve a maximum transfer rate of 1200 bps—2400 (the baud rate) divided by 2 (the number of baud required to transmit 1 bit).

While all this technical gobbledygook might be interesting, understanding precisely what it means is not mandatory to successfully establish a connection between two modems. All you need to know is whether your modem can match the transmission rate of any modem to which you connect. This is critical. A modem with a maximum baud rate of 1200, for example, cannot communicate with a modem transmitting at 2400-baud any more than a person who speaks only English can talk with someone who does not understand that language.

Even this potential problem, however, is largely overcome by the advanced design of newer modems. Today's modems support multiple transmission speeds, with their listed baud rate being the fastest speed at which they can operate. A 2400-baud modem, therefore, should also be able to handle 1200- and 300-baud sessions without a hitch. Consequently (and helped along by the fact that their prices have dropped noticeably over the past year or so), 2400-baud modems are now almost standard for PC communications. If you're looking to buy a modem, therefore, a 2400-baud model is a pretty safe bet.

Where It's AT

A third factor to consider when choosing a modem is the method it uses to recognize commands sent from your PC (i.e., whether or not it is compatible with your communications software). Let's face it, the PC industry is infamous for a lack of standards. There's no guarantee a monitor from one company will work properly with a display card manufactured by one of its competitors. Even though the same 3 1/2-inch diskette fits in a disk drive on either an Apple Macintosh and IBM PS/2, the methods used by these two systems to read and write information to and from that diskette differ radically. Sometimes, in fact, different products from the same manufacturer are incompatible with one another, as is the case when a single company produces hardware components for both Macintosh and MS-DOS computers.

Against all odds, however, a de facto "standard" of sorts has emerged for modem communications. The "Hayes AT command set" pretty much rules the roost in the modem marketplace.

This command set derives its name from the convention of preceding all instructions to your modem with the two-letter code *AT*, to let it know that a command is coming—to get its *AT*tention, so to speak. (For example, the AT command *ATDP* tells your modem: "ATtention, prepare to Dial the phone, using the Pulse method.") If the modem you are considering is Hayes-compatible, it should recognize the AT command set—a definite plus, since this is the command set used by the vast majority of communications programs currently on the market. (The AT commands will be examined in greater detail in a later chapter.)

Speaking of communications programs, let's close down our discussion of hardware and take a closer look at the type of software you need to telecommunicate.

37

Selecting the Right Software

Choosing the best software to meet your on-line needs is no easy task, especially if you've never used your PC to communicate with another computer. The wealth of features and functions available in many of today's programs can easily confuse the novice, who is unfamiliar with what telecommunications is and how it works.

As is true of many specialized activities, individuals who telecommunicate with any regularity speak a language all their own. Over the past few years, a virtual dictionary of dedicated terms has developed around this application area. DTR, scripts, auto-answer, host mode, CR/LF translation, terminal emulation: these are but a few of the esoteric buzzwords you will encounter when you begin investigating communications software. Once you understand what these terms mean, using them becomes habit. When you're first getting your feet wet in modem communications, however, they tend to confuse the real issue of how to pick the program that's right for you.

Let's begin by identifying the two primary functions a communications program must perform:

1. It has to be able to establish a connection with another computer.
2. It must be able to coordinate its own activities with those of the other computer, once such a connection is made.

In truth, any software that can accomplish these two tasks can be used to telecommunicate. A good communications program, however, allows much more.

Let Your Modem Do the Dialing

One way to simplify the actual process of connecting your PC with another computer is to choose a communications program which includes some sort of Dialing Directory feature.

Basically, a Dialing Directory allows you to specify important information about any remote system you plan to connect with on a regular basis, such as its telephone number, the communications settings (baud rate, parity, etc.), and the like. Once this information is recorded in the Dialing Directory, connecting with a given system becomes a simple matter of identifying which directory listing you wish to access and then, telling your communications program to call it. Prior to placing this call, the software automatically adjusts all appropriate settings to those specified for the selected directory listing, without your having to make these changes manually.

Follow the Script

Another convenient feature to look for in a communications program is some type of script or macro language. When such a feature is available, it can automate many of your on-line activities.

For example, you could write a script to dial a remote system, enter any information required to identify you as being a registered user of that system (your user ID and password), check to see if there are messages waiting for you on that system and, should any exist, retrieve those messages to store them in a disk file on your PC where you could read and review at your convenience. Some communications programs even include script languages that allow you to initiate these steps automatically at a predetermined time—for instance, late at night, when long-distance rates are low—without your having to be there to actually start the process.

The best advice I can offer is this: If possible, buy a communications program that supports a comprehensive script language. Even if you don't fully understand how scripts work now, you'll be glad you included this in your "must have" features list later.

The Return of the AT Commands

Make certain the communications software you buy uses the Hayes AT command set to communicate with your modem. In truth, virtually all communications software supports the AT command set. The critical point here is to make sure you don't accidentally pick up one of the rare programs still on the market that employs a command set other than the Hayes standard.

Diagnose the Documentation

39

If possible, try to examine the manuals for any communications software you are considering before actually plunking down your hard-earned shekels for it. The process of connecting your PC with another computer is complicated. You shouldn't have to rely on a manual filled with "technobabble" and buzzwords to figure out how to accomplish this. Rather, try to find a program whose manual clearly describes what you are doing, and how you do it, in plain English.

These are merely some practical features to look for in a communications program. Beyond this, of course, choose software that will not only meet your current needs, but will grow with you. Sure, you may own a 2400-baud modem now, but it's possible that somewhere down the line you will upgrade to a faster model. It would be nice, therefore, to have your current communications software support a 9600-baud modem, should you buy one sometime in the future. In other words, try to anticipate tomorrow's upgrades in the communications software you buy today. In doing so, you are not forced to replace a program you've already learned each time your needs change.

So, the natural question becomes: Are there any communications programs I can recommend? Yes, but you must know that the programs listed here merely represent the ones with which I am familiar enough to recommend. Certainly, other competent packages exist.

I must admit I'm partial to ProComm Plus (Datastorm Technologies, P.O. Box 1471, Columbia, Missouri 65205, 314-443-3282). So much so, in fact, that I've not only used this program for years, but I recently wrote a book about it, *The First Book of Procomm Plus*, for the same company (SAMS, a division of Macmillan Computer Publishing) publishing this book. It is an inexpensive program that provides power and special features. The Procomm Plus Dialing Directory is not only flexible, it's also easy to set up and use. (See Figure 3.3.) The program's powerful script language can automate virtually any on-line activity, no matter how complex. As an added attraction, Procomm Plus includes a Host mode feature, which allows you to set up your PC to function much like a bulletin board system (BBS). In the Host mode, you can call up your computer to transfer files, read and leave messages, and even execute certain DOS commands from a remote PC.

40

```
DIALING DIRECTORY: BOSTON

      NAME                           NUMBER       BAUD P D S D   SCRIPT
   1  BOSTON AREA BBS SYSTEMS                     1200 N-8-1 F
   2  ------------------------------             1200 N-8-1 F
   3  Alpha Software           1 617 229-2915     2400 N-8-1 F
   4  Bald Eagle               1 617 494-2985     1200 N-8-1 F
   5  Base 10                  1 617 721-7360     2400 N-8-1 F
   6  BCSNET Host              1 617 964-2546     2400 N-8-1 F
   7  BINEX II                 1 617 326-0259     2400 N-8-1 F
   8  Bionic Dog               1 617 964-8069     1200 N-8-1 F
   9  BIX                      1 617 861-9767     1200 N-8-1 F
  10  Blue Line                1 617 721-1688     2400 N-8-1 F

   PgUp Scroll Up    ↑/↓ Select Entry     R Revise Entry      C Clear Marked
   PgDn Scroll Dn    Space Mark Entry     E Erase Entry(s)    L Print Directory
   Home First Page   Enter Dial Selected  F Find Entry        P Dialing Codes
   End Last Page     D Dial Entry(s)      A Find Again        X Exchange Dir
   Esc Exit          M Manual Dial        G Goto Entry        T Toggle Display

   Choice:

   PORT: COM1   SETTINGS: 2400 N-8-1    DUPLEX: FULL   DIALING CODES:
```

Figure 3.3 Procomm Plus includes a flexible Dialing Directory.

Another MS-DOS program I highly recommend is CrossTalk (Digital Communications Associates, Inc., 1000 Alderman Drive, Alpharetta, Georgia, 30202, (800)241-4762). CrossTalk has been among the top selling DOS communications programs for years. You don't stay successful that long without having something going for you. CrossTalk possesses the added attraction of being available in several different versions. One such version, CrossTalk for Windows, is designed to run under Windows 3.0, the graphics-based operating environment that's currently taking the MS-DOS market by storm.

A second impressive Windows-based communications program is Microphone II (Software Ventures Corporation, 2907 Claremont Ave., Suite 220, Berkeley, CA 94705, 415-644-3232). MicroPhone II ships with several preprogrammed scripts designed to simplify the process of signing onto several popular commercial on-line information systems (CompuServe, BIX, Dow Jones, MCI Mail, and GEnie, among others). When you load a script for one of these services the first time, clicking on a special Profile button causes MicroPhone II to display a series of prompts requesting the information it needs to connect you to that service—access number, your user ID, your password, and the like. The Profile button is also used to change any of these items, as would be required, for example, if you moved and had to use a different access number to contact a given service. Like many Windows-based programs, Microphone II started on the Macintosh side of the PC fence. Consequently, it's a logical choice for anyone who uses both of these popular PC platforms during the course of their daily work.

As I said, there are other, equally competent communications programs out there. The key is to find the one that best meets your needs (using the criteria outlined earlier) and most closely matches the way you like to work.

41

Reach Out and Touch

The final, most necessary item is a phone line. This is so obvious, that you may believe there isn't much to discuss here. Either you already have a telephone line available, or you simply call the phone company and get one installed. Still, there are a couple of points you should be aware of to avoid problems down the road.

The Call-Waiting Blues

First, beware of the Call-Waiting feature most phone companies offer. Although convenient for voice communications, Call Waiting can wreak havoc on a telecommunications session. The beep that heralds an incoming call immediately drops your data connection, thus interrupting whatever activity you were performing at the time.

This need not be a hopeless situation, however. Depending on the type of equipment your phone company uses, you can temporarily suspend Call Waiting whenever you place a phone call with your modem.

To test whether this is true for your phone system, pick up your phone and press the pound sign (#), followed by 70. If you receive a second dial tone, then your phone company uses newer equipment that allows you to temporarily suspend Call Waiting. (If you place a call now, anyone attempting to reach you during that call will receive a busy signal. Don't worry, Call Waiting goes back into effect when you finish the current call.) If you don't have a phone line, find out whether or not this feature is available when you contact the local phone company to schedule installation. To take advantage of this feature for your communications activities, simply precede each connection you make with a *#70* sequence, either manually or by adding this code to the beginning of the Dialing Directory entries in your communications program.

42

> ▶ **Note:** Entering an alternate code, 1170, is often used to defeat Call Waiting on older, pulse-dialing systems. The real trick here is to contact your local telephone company to see if it offers Call Waiting and the ability to defeat that convenience, when appropriate.

A Better Solution, Get a Second Line

You may want to consider installing a second, dedicated phone line for your modem communications. In addition to eliminating any problems you may encounter with Call Waiting, if it's installed on your main line, having a dedicated modem line can be convenient. Many times I've had troubles arise during a communications session. However, each time I was able to resolve them by simply calling the other party on my voice line.

Protecting Your Investment

Your PC and modem can represent a sizable financial investment. It only makes sense, therefore, to protect them against accidental damage. The biggest threat to any computer hardware is a *power surge*, a sudden and sporadic change in the electrical current flowing from a wall outlet or even across a telephone line.

Many multi-outlet power strips include built-in surge-suppressor circuitry, which protects any equipment plugged into them from being damaged by power fluctuations in your electrical line. Installing one of these relatively inexpensive devices in your PC system can help you avoid a costly repair somewhere down the line (pun intended).

You use a standard telephone cord (called an *RJ-11 cord*) to connect your modem to a phone jack or wall plug, much as you would a typical modular telephone. When installing your modem, protect it with a telephone-line surge protector (Figure 3.4) to guard against any voltage spikes or power surges originating in the telephone lines.

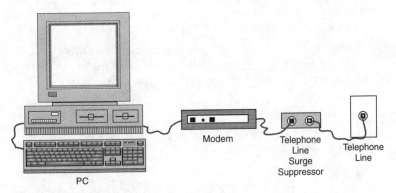

Figure 3.4 A typical external modem setup, including a telephone-line surge protector.

> ⊘ **Caution:** Even with a power-line surge supressor and telephone-line protector installed on your PC, it's always a good idea to unplug both your computer system and RJ-11 telephone cord during a thunderstorm. Though useful for controlling common fluctuations in power and telephone lines, no manmade protector can stand up to the unbridled fury of Mother Nature.

Now that you know what you need to telecommunicate, the next step is to install and set up these items. In the next chapter we'll start putting all the pieces together. We'll begin by using your PC, modem, and communications software to contact other computers.

What You Have Learned

▶ Modem communications require only a minimum amount of physical equipment. Basically, anyone with a personal computer and a modem can telecommunicate.

▶ A communications program is a special type of software that allows you to control your modem and manage on-line sessions. Features you should look for in a good communications program include a Dialing Directory, a script language, and support for the standard AT command set.

▶ As a rule, it's a good idea to install a dedicated telephone line for your modem. If a dedicated line is not available, take the necessary steps to ensure that Call Waiting, a popular feature on today's phone lines, does not interrupt your on-line sessions.

▶ Using an outlet strip with surge-suppressor circuitry and installing a surge protector between your modem and telephone line can protect your equipment against damage from power fluctuations.

Chapter 4

Setting Up To Telecommunicate

45

In This Chapter

- ▶ Installing a modem
- ▶ Configuring a modem to work properly with your PC
- ▶ Installing a communications program
- ▶ Setting up a communications program to work properly with your modem

Throughout the first three chapters of this book, we introduced how critical it is to understand what modems are and how they work. However, this introductory material did little to increase your knowledge of the specific steps required to begin actually using a modem and your PC to communicate with other computers. In this chapter, we'll start getting down to the "nitty-gritty" of telecommunications by beginning to look at what's involved in installing and setting up a modem and communications program to work properly on your PC.

Modem Installation

As explained in the previous chapter, PC modems can be grouped into two major categories: internal modems and external modems.

Once installed, internal and external modems are virtually identical to one another in what they do and how they do it. However, the exact procedures used to set up your modem differ, depending on what type of modem it is. We'll begin by looking at the steps involved in adding an internal modem to your PC.

Installing an Internal Modem

As its name implies, an internal modem is installed *inside* your PC. Now, I can almost hear you thinking: "Inside my PC? As in remove the cover from my system and actually add a piece of hardware to it? You must be kidding!" I'm not. Thanks to the foresight of the people who designed the original IBM personal computer, though, this isn't as difficult as it sounds.

46

> **Caution:** You should always turn off your computer and unplug its power cord before installing any new equipment in it. Not only does this stop a stray spark or two from damaging your system, but it also prevents a simple installation procedure from turning into a truly shocking experience, if you get my drift. Also, you should avoid discharging static electricity into your system. (A small spark carries the wallop of a lightening bolt on the relatively small scale of PC components.) One good way to avoid this is by touching your fingertip to a metallic object like a doorknob or file cabinet before actually reaching into your PC.

Removing Your System Cover

Many of today's most popular computers can be easily modified, their native capabilities enhanced simply by adding a new piece of equipment, called a *peripheral*, to them. This is especially true if your personal computer uses the MS-DOS operating system—that is, if it is an IBM or IBM-compatible PC.

Recognizing that people's needs—as well as the PC equipment they need to use—can change over time, the makers of the original IBM PC designed it to include a built-in *expansion bus*. As a rule, this expansion bus consists of a series of slots lined up along the back of the system's *motherboard* (Figure 4.1), a special board containing your PC's primary components (BIOS and memory chips, electrical connections, etc.). By inserting different types of *expansion cards* into these slots, you can improve your system's performance, endowing it with features it would not otherwise possess (such as extra memory, a better video display, external storage devices, etc.). Installing an internal modem card into one of these expansion slots enhances your system by adding telecommunications to your PC arsenal.

Motherboard Expansion Slots Input/Output (I/O) Ports Microprocessor (CPU)

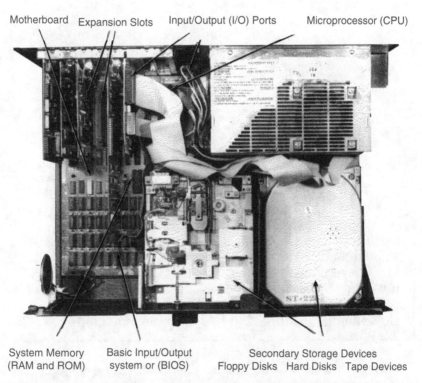

System Memory   Basic Input/Output   Secondary Storage Devices
(RAM and ROM)   system or (BIOS)   Floppy Disks Hard Disks Tape Devices

Figure 4.1 One way to modify an IBM-compatible PC is by installing special cards into its built-in expansion slots.

Of course, placing something inside a PC requires opening it up first. In other words, you must remove its system cover to access its built-in expansion slots. This usually involves removing several screws located on the back panel of the main system unit, as illustrated in Figure 4.2.

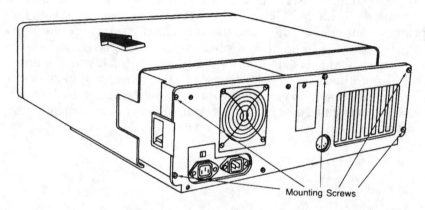

*Figure 4.2 **Several screws are removed from the back panel to open your system.***

Mounting Screws

48

> ▶ **Note:** Not all PCs are created equal. Nor are they designed identically to one another. Figure 4.2 shows a typical IBM-compatible desktop unit that uses standard screws to secure its system cover. Some newer models replace these standard screws with special thumbscrews. The advantage to the thumb-screw design is that you don't need a screwdriver to remove your system cover. Another variation on the desktop theme is the recent emergence of *tower systems*, PC units designed to stand directly on the floor rather than be placed on a desktop. Most tower systems include a side panel, which slides off to reveal their internal components. Regardless of what type of PC you own, the specific procedures used to access its expansion slots should be outlined in its system documentation.

After these screws are removed, you should be able to slide the system cover off your PC. To do so, slowly pull the cover toward you. (Be careful that none of the internal wires or connectors get entangled in the system cover as you remove it.) With the system cover removed, you can see the inside of your PC—which, if it is a desktop model, will resemble Figure 4.1. Notice the expansion slots lined up across the back of the motherboard. The first thing you need to do is identify an empty slot suitable for installing your internal modem.

> ⊘ **Caution:** Removing the system cover from your PC exposes it to a variety of potentially damaging environmental hazards: lint, dust, cigarette ashes, jewelry, a stray paper clip, even a human hair. Although there's no need to set up a sterile environment similar to those clean rooms and laboratories seen in scientific reports on the news, care should be taken to keep such contaminants away from delicate system components while the inside of your PC is exposed to the world.

Picking an Expansion Slot

Figure 4.3 shows a typical internal modem card. An internal modem doesn't look that different from any other PC expansion card. Notice the row of gold-plated connectors protruding from the bottom of this card. Special care should be taken not to touch these connectors, which slide into the expansion slot, during modem installation. They transfer information in the form of electrical signals back and forth between the modem card and your PC's motherboard. Dust, dirt, or fingerprints can result in a poor connection and interfere with this process.

49

Figure 4.3 A typical internal modem card.

Depending on what type of PC you own, the motherboard contains expansion slots of several different sizes. Due to the design of the Intel 8088 and 8086 CPUs used in the original IBM PC (and compatible systems), data is transferred through the expansion slots built into these early units in 8-bit chunks only.

Beginning with IBM's second-generation AT system, a personal computer built around Intel's 80286 CPU, it became possible to transfer data to and from an expansion card 16 bits at a time, or at approximately twice the transfer rate supported by earlier PC/XT models. To accommodate this increased data-transfer rate, larger expansion slots were incorporated into the motherboard of the AT and compatible systems. Although expansion cards supporting 8-bit data transfer can be inserted into a 16-bit AT slot, the opposite is not true. (Imagine trying to stuff ten pounds of potatoes into a five-pound bag, and you'll get a rough idea of why this is so.)

Most internal modem cards still use the earlier, 8-bit PC/XT design. However, some newer, hybrid models (e.g., an expansion card that combines modem and FAX capabilities on a single card) require a 16-bit slot to work properly. As a rule, the most logical approach is to install your modem card in the smallest expansion slot with which it is compatible. This leaves your larger slots free to accept other, more powerful expansion cards sometime in the future.

Preparing an Expansion Slot for Use

Once you've selected an expansion slot for your internal modem, the next step is to remove the plate most manufacturers include in their system design to protect unoccupied slots against dust and other contaminates. To eliminate this protective plate, remove its anchor screw, as illustrated in Figure 4.4. Set this screw aside in a safe place. You'll use it later to securely fasten the modem card to your PC.

After removing the anchor screw, lift the protective plate (i.e., slide it carefully out of the backplane slot into which it was inserted) to insert your modem card into the expansion slot. As you've probably noticed by now, the internal modem is mounted on a plate similar to the one you just removed. Use this plate to anchor the modem card to your PC following installation.

Inserting the Modem Card

The next step is to actually insert the internal modem into your PC. The best way to accomplish this is to first position the modem card's mounting plate against your PC's backplane, taking care to hold the card only by its edges. Next, carefully slide this plate down into the

50

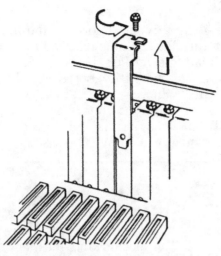

Figure 4.4 *Protective plates prevent dust and other contaminates from getting into unused expansion slots.*

51

motherboard. This positions the front section of the modem card's
connector pins into the expansion slot. Then, gently but firmly press
against the middle of the modem card until the remaining connector
pins are inserted into the expansion slot.

After installing the modem card within your PC, be sure to replace
and tighten the anchor screw you removed from the original protective
plate. This prevents your modem card from detaching itself from the
expansion bus, as could happen over time if the modem plate is not
firmly anchored to your system's backplane.

Once everything is in place, you can replace your system cover.
(Once again, be careful not to ensnare any wires while doing so.) After
you reassemble your PC, the only task left undone is actually plugging
your modem into the phone line. Before getting into that, however, let's
walk through the steps involved in adding an external modem to a PC,
for those readers who own one.

Installing an External Modem

To hook up an external modem, you need a few extra pieces of
equipment that are not required for an internal modem. To begin with,
make certain your system includes at least one external *serial port*. A
serial port is a special input/output device that your computer uses to
communicate with the peripherals that are not inserted directly into an
expansion slot on its motherboard.

> ▶ **Note:** Quite often, this serial port is mounted on a special card that, in turn, needs to be inserted into your system's expansion bus. Many newer PCs, however, have all the electronic circuitry associated with a serial port built into their motherboard. If this is the case, an external connector for this serial port will be located somewhere on your system cabinet. If not specifically labeled as a serial port, this external connector may be identified as COM1 or COM2.

Cable Confusion

In addition to a serial port, a special cable is required to connect an external modem to a PC. The specific kind of cable you need for your system depends on what type of connector its serial port has.

There are two distinct types of serial port connectors, as illustrated in Figure 4.5:

▶ 9-pin adapters

▶ 25-pin adapters

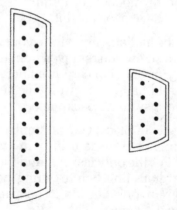

Figure 4.5 An external serial port can use either a 9- or 25-pin connector.

Everyone who figured out that the primary difference between these two connectors is how many pins each contains, raise their right hand. (See how easy telecommunications can be.) External modems are generally equipped with a 25-pin connector. As a rule, therefore, you need one of the following two cable types to connect an external modem to your PC:

▶ If the serial port on your PC uses a 9-pin connector, you need a serial cable with a 9-pin adapter on one end, the end that connects to your PC, and a 25-pin adapter which is plugged into the external modem.

▶ If the serial port on your PC uses a 25-pin connector, you need a serial cable with a 25-pin adapter on each end.

A Brief Course in Sex Education

Connectors and cables come in specific genders, vis-a-vis, male and female. A connector or cable containing the actual pins used to transmit electronic signals between your PC and an external device is called the *male adapter*. Conversely, a connector or cable containing holes into which these pins are inserted is called a *female adapter*.

The rule here is simple. If the serial port on your PC has a male connector, as most do, then you need a female adapter on the end of the serial cable that connects to it. Because most modems are equipped with 25-pin female connectors, a male adapter is required at the modem end of the serial cable used to attach an external modem to your PC.

In all likelihood, therefore, you will need one of the following two cable types to connect an external modem to your PC:

▶ 9-pin female to 25-pin male serial cable

▶ 25-pin female to 25-pin male serial cable

Of course, every rule has its exceptions. The important thing is that you understand the difference between male and female connectors and the corresponding cable adapters. If you do, you should be able to purchase the appropriate cable for your PC and external modem.

Powering Up Your Modem

Unlike an internal modem, which pulls the minimal power it requires to operate directly from your PC's expansion bus, an external modem must be plugged into an electrical outlet. Most external modems include an AC/DC adapter for this purpose. (Modems require low-voltage DC power, as opposed to the 110-volt AC current generated by a standard outlet.) Setting up an external modem to work with your PC, therefore, is a two-step process:

1. Use the appropriate serial cable to connect the external modem to either your COM1 or COM2 serial port.

2. Use the modem's AC/DC adapter to provide it with electrical current.

53

Connecting Your Modem to a Phone Line

At this point, your modem is almost ready to use, regardless of whether it is in internal or external model. All that remains now is to actually hook your modem up to a telephone line.

I'm going to assume here that you have a modular phone jack (also called an RJ11 plug) installed in your home or office, similar to the one shown in Figure 4.6. If this is not the case, you need special equipment to make the connection between your modem and the phone system. The specific equipment required depends on the type phone hookup you have.

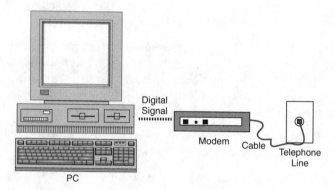

Figure 4.6 Most modems use a standard RJ11 telephone cord to connect them to the phone system.

Basically, you connect a modem to your phone line the same way you plug in a standard telephone, by inserting one end of the RJ11 cord into the modem and the other end into a modular wall jack. That's all there is to it.

> ▶ **Tip:** Some modems include two RJ11 plugs, one marked *LINE* and a second marked *PHONE*. With this arrangement, it's possible to *daisy chain* both your modem and a standard telephone (or answering machine, if you want) off of a single modular wall jack. To do so, simply use the RJ11 cord provided with your modem to connect it to the wall jack, inserting that cord into the plug marked LINE. Next, plug your regular telephone into the second RJ11 connector, the one marked PHONE. Doing so causes your phone to operate just as if it were plugged directly into the wall jack.

Configuring Your Modem

Congratulations! Regardless of whether you own an internal or external modem, it should now be ready to use. Well, almost ready to use. You still need to fine tune its performance to match your PC hardware.

Many modems include *DIP switches*—(a tiny row of on/off switches that somewhat resemble little teeth). Figure 4.7 shows a typical bank of DIP switches. Where these switches are located and what they accomplish vary from modem to modem. For example, an internal modem's DIP switches can be located either on the modem board itself or mounted so that they're able to be accessed through its mounting plate. (The latter arrangement is more convenient, since it does not require that you remove the modem board to adjust its default configuration.) Similarly, although the DIP switches for most external modems are located on the back of the unit, some models vary from this design.

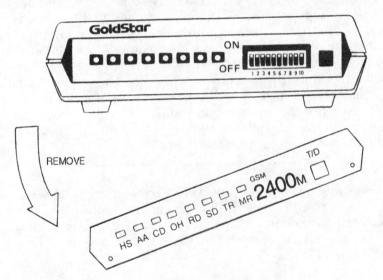

Figure 4.7 A modem's DIP switches are used to specify its default configuration.

The setting of individual DIP switches determines whether it automatically answers any incoming calls, how it responds to commands during an on-line session, and the speed at which it normally operates. How many switches there are, and what each does, varies from modem to modem. Within these variations, however, certain consistencies do exist, specifically in the configuration options that the DIP switches allow you to specify. For example, virtually all modems have a DIP switch that allows you to specify whether they should be configured to run in synchronous and asynchronous communications mode. (In case you're wondering, most PC-to-PC communications utilize asynchronous procedures, which we'll discuss later.) Another common default setting specified with a DIP switch is one that allows you to indicate whether the modem should automatically respond to any incoming calls it receives, commonly referred to as an *Auto-Answer feature*. Unfortunately, beyond pointing out these relatively universal examples, about the only thing I can tell you with any certainty is that your modem's documentation should describe those configuration settings it does support, as well as explain where its DIP switches are located and how they work.

> ▶ **Note:** Baseball's great Yogi Berra posited a rule of thumb I'd like to pass on: "If it ain't broke, don't fix it." Most modems are preconfigured by their manufacturer to handle the vast majority of PC-to-PC communications. Also, the operational settings specified with DIP switches are often changed "on the fly," from within a communications program. A special command is usually available, for example, to switch your modem over to auto-answer mode, if necessary. Unless you encounter a recurring problem when first using your modem, therefore, you'll probably never need to mess around with its DIP switches. Still, it's a good idea to have at least a basic understanding of where to find them and how they are used, just in case.

Now that we've outlined the various steps involved in hooking up a modem to your PC, why don't we jump over to the software side of the communications fence? Specifically, let's look at how to install and set up a communications program (the software used to manage your on-line activities).

Software Installation

As I pointed out in the previous chapter, communications programs abound in the PC marketplace. These programs differ greatly; both in their appearance and, to a lesser degree, the capabilities they support. Still, the primary function of a communications program is universal, regardless of which package you choose. A communications program is designed to let you issue the commands that tell your modem what to do and how to do it.

Don't let the word *commands* scare you. Through the years, computers have developed a reputation for being difficult—no, make that impossible—to use. In the beginning of the computer revolution, this reputation may have been well deserved. Back then, computers were highly specialized machines run by highly trained specialists. Recently, however, and especially since the introduction of the PC, the computer has emigrated from the exclusive domain of experts and eccentrics and assumed its rightful place in the mainstream of society.

For this assimilation to succeed, the people in charge of such matters had to simplify matters from the way they were in those early days of the computer age to make computer hardware and software more accessible to the masses. For the most part, they have succeeded. Though still not as easy to use as a toaster (and feel free to argue with anybody, especially a computer salesperson, who tells you that they are), PC programs, including most communications packages, have at least evolved to the point where you no longer need a doctorate in computer sciences to get them up and running on your system.

Copy vs. Install

The first thing to determine is what steps are required to prepare your software for use. Some communications programs run as is, right out of the box. To prepare such programs for use, simply copy their program files from the original distribution diskettes to work disks or, alternately, your hard disk. Other packages include a special installation program that you must run before they work properly. The latter would be the case, for example, if a manufacturer compressed its program files to cut down on the number (and, therefore, the cost) of disks used to distribute its product. Before using such a package, you need to expand any compressed files its distribution disks contain into executable programs.

It would be impossible for me to outline the specific installation steps required for every communications program currently available. There are literally hundreds of them from which to choose. Describing some of the more common pieces of information you'll be asked to provide during installation, however, will help you prepare for this critical step in getting your PC and modem ready to telecommunicate.

57

Specifying Default Settings

As a rule, the Installation utility of your communications program displays a special screen or series of screens that you can use to tell it how you want your PC, modem, and communications software to coordinate the majority of your on-line session (i.e., the *default settings* that are assigned to your program). Figure 4.8, for example, shows the Program Setup screen that one popular MS-DOS communications package, Procomm Plus, uses to request its default settings.

```
┌──────────────────────────────────────────────────────────────────┐
│ PROCOMM PLUS INSTALLATION UTILITY              PROGRAM STARTUP SETTINGS │
│                                                                    │
│    Monitor:                      Monitor:                          │
│      Modem:                                                        │
│   Terminal:                         1- Color                       │
│  Comm Port:                         2- Composite B&W               │
│  Baud Rate:                         3- Monochrome                  │
│     Parity:                                                        │
│  Data Bits:                                                        │
│  Stop Bits:                                                        │
│      Duplex:                                                       │
│   Protocol:                                                        │
│                                                                    │
│ ┌ MONITOR ─────────────────────────────────────────────────────  │
│                                                                    │
│ Specify the type of monitor that you are using.  Select COLOR if you are │
│ using a color monitor with a color graphics card.  PROCOMM PLUS will come │
│ alive in a blaze of exciting colors.  Select COMPOSITE B&W if you have a │
│ black and white composite monitor with a graphics card.  Select MONOCHROME │
│ if you are using a monochrome monitor with a monochrome dislay card. │
│            ** Press ESC to exit, or any other key to begin **      │
└──────────────────────────────────────────────────────────────────┘
```

Figure 4.8 While installing a communications program, you're generally given an opportunity to specify default settings for your on-line activities.

Specifying the default settings for most programs is a relatively straightforward procedure. Again, by way of an example, Procomm Plus employs the screen shown in Figure 4.8 to let you enter the number for each setting that is most appropriate for your hardware configuration or communications preferences. The Procomm Plus Setup utility then stores your settings each time you start the program. Other communications programs may use a different procedure, but the underlying concept is the same.

Values commonly specified during installation include:

▶ *Monitor.* The type of monitor installed on your system.

▶ *Modem.* The type of modem installed on your system.

▶ *Terminal.* The type of terminal you want your PC to emulate during a communications session.

▶ *Comm Port.* The communications (COM) or serial port to which you connected your modem while installing it on your system.

▶ *Baud Rate.* The default speed (or bps) at which your modem transmits data to a remote computer during a communications session.

The value you enter here should be the highest baud rate supported by your modem. On a Hayes 2400 Smartmodem, for example, this would be 2400 baud.

▶ *Parity.* The method used to test the validity of data transmitted during a communications session. Unless you know it should be set differently, a good default value for the Parity field is None.

▶ *Data Bits.* How many bits (binary digits) used to represent one character during a communications session. Unless you know it should be set differently, a good default value for the Data Bits field is 8.

▶ *Stop Bits.* How many bits are used to indicate a complete character has been transmitted during a communications session. Unless you know it should be set differently, a good default value for the Stop Bits field is 1.

▶ *Duplex.* Sometimes called *Echo,* the duplex setting determines whether characters you type at your keyboard are sent directly to your display screen (half-duplex) or first transmitted to the remote system and then returned to your monitor (full-duplex). Unless you know it should be set differently, a good default value for the Duplex field is *full.*

▶ *Protocol.* Protocol defines how your PC and a remote computer manages file transfers. Explaining the specifics of every file-transfer protocol would require a highly technical discussion, which is beyond the scope of this book. However, it is important to know that both computers must use the same protocol for a file transfer to be successful. Most programs provide you with the opportunity to specify a different protocol than your default setting prior to beginning a file transfer. A good default protocol is XMODEM, one of the most universal protocols available for transferring binary files.

59

▶ **Note:** Don't worry if you don't completely understand what these terms mean at this point. All will be explained as we progress through this book. Also, most programs allow you to easily modify your default settings later, if necessary. Appendix C of this book outlines some of the problems you can encounter, should one or more of your default settings be entered incorrectly.

After specifying the default settings in Procomm Plus, your screen should resemble Figure 4.9. (For this exercise, I selected the default settings mentioned above. Your screen may differ slightly from Figure 4.9, depending on what program you use and the settings you specify.)

60

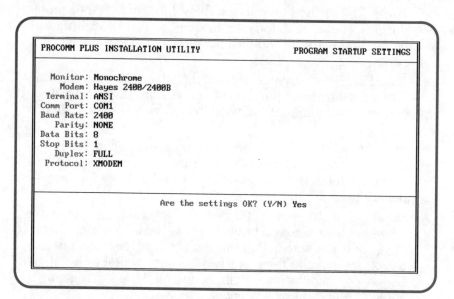

```
PROCOMM PLUS INSTALLATION UTILITY          PROGRAM STARTUP SETTINGS

   Monitor: Monochrome
     Modem: Hayes 2400/2400B
  Terminal: ANSI
 Comm Port: COM1
 Baud Rate: 2400
    Parity: NONE
 Data Bits: 8
 Stop Bits: 1
    Duplex: FULL
  Protocol: XMODEM



                 Are the settings OK? (Y/N) Yes
```

Figure 4.9 This screen shows some common values you might specify for your default communications settings, using Procomm Plus as an example.

Remember, every communications program has its own installation procedure. Some programs request information about the modem and communications environment during installation, as Procomm Plus does. Others provide a special setup utility to run after the actual program files have been installed on your system in order to define default parameters for your on-line activities. At this time, the important thing to remember is that the values you specify should be those used most often. Also, don't worry if you make a mistake and enter an incorrect value in your initial configuration. Any communications program worth using allows you to modify its default settings with relative ease, as you become more familiar with how it works and more cognizant of the kind of work you normally do, when you go on-line. Despite the bad rap they regularly must endure, PCs and the programs they run are not really as unforgiving as many people believe.

Specifying a Dial Command

The parameters outlined in the previous section are the primary settings to be concerned with when initially configuring your communications software. They are, after all, critical to having your modem work properly. Consequently, most programs ask you to specify these values at some time during installation. However, there are additional items to consider when setting up your communications environment.

I briefly introduced the AT commands in the previous chapter, but we'll discuss them in greater detail in the next chapter. At this time, however, I need to talk a little bit about a very important AT command used to specify the technique your modem should use to "dial the telephone."

As you may recall, I proposed that telecommunications would be easier if hardware and software were standardized in the PC world. Well, now you can add the telephone system used to connect your PC with a remote system to the list of the nonstandardized items that adversely affect telecommunications. Despite a common belief that a single telephone network grids our country, there are really two types of systems out there: those that support touch-tone dialing and those that don't.

Although the former, the more modern touch-tone system, is considered state-of-the-art and the preferred paradigm, some parts of the country have not yet upgraded to this new standard. In these areas, outdated switching equipment forces the local phone company to rely on the older, pulse dialing method. The AT Dial command allows you to specify which technique your modem should use when placing calls from your PC.

61

Remember, the AT command set derives its name from the fact that you precede instructions sent to a modem from your PC with the letters AT, a special code designed to get the modem's ATtention. The AT command to have your modem dial a number on a touch-tone phone system is *ATDT* (ATtention Dial Tone). On a *pulse dialing system* (i.e., a phone system that does not support touch-tone dialing) the corresponding command is *ATDP* (ATtention Dial Pulse).

Your communications programs should provide some method for specifying which command is compatible with the local phone system. Returning to our previous example of Procomm Plus, for instance, you do this by entering the appropriate AT Dial command into one of the fields listed under the Modem options of its Setup utility, as illustrated in Figure 4.10. To avoid potential problems, you should check your program's manual to find out what procedure it uses to specify the AT Dial command, and then make sure this value is set correctly immediately following installation.

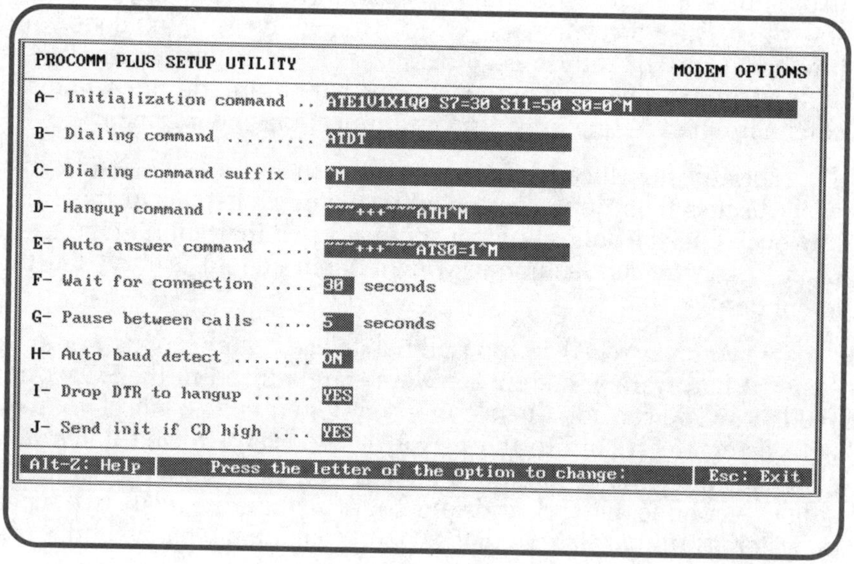

62

```
PROCOMM PLUS SETUP UTILITY                                    MODEM OPTIONS

A- Initialization command .. ATE1V1X1Q0 S7=30 S11=50 S0=0^M

B- Dialing command ........ ATDT

C- Dialing command suffix .. ^M

D- Hangup command ......... ~~~+++~~~ATH^M

E- Auto answer command ..... ~~~+++~~~ATS0=1^M

F- Wait for connection ..... 30  seconds

G- Pause between calls ..... 5   seconds

H- Auto baud detect ........ ON

I- Drop DTR to hangup ...... YES

J- Send init if CD high .... YES

Alt-Z: Help  |  Press the letter of the option to change:  | Esc: Exit
```

Figure 4.10 Most communications programs allow you to specify an AT Dial command that is compatible with your local phone system.

▶ **Note:** If you're not sure what type of system your local phone company uses, you can always specify the ATDP command. All touch-tone systems are also capable of supporting pulse dialing.

At this point, your modem and communications program are installed and ready to use. Certainly, you'll fine-tune your on-line environment over time, as you become more familiar with how modem communications work. What you have now, however, is the basic equipment (hardware and software) needed to telecommunicate. And that's exactly what we'll do in the next chapter, as you make your first on-line connection with these newly installed tools.

What You Have Learned

- ▶ Internal and external modems are virtually identical to one another in what they do and how they do it, once one is installed on your system. The exact procedures used to set up your modem differ, however, depending on what type of modem you own.

- ▶ Many personal computers can be easily modified by installing special cards within their built-in expansion bus, usually a series of slots located on the system's motherboard. The expansion bus is used to install an internal modem card in your PC.

- ▶ To install an external modem on your PC, it must include at least one external serial or COM port. You need the appropriate serial cable to connect an external modem to this port.

- ▶ You use a communications program to issue the commands that make your modem perform a specific activity. During installation you'll generally specify the communications parameters — serial port, baud rate, parity, and the like — your communications program should use at the default settings for your on-line environment.

- ▶ The ATD (Dial) command is used to indicate whether your modem should use touch-tone dialing or the older pulse-dialing technique to place calls on your local phone system.

63

Chapter 5

Making That First Connection

In This Chapter

▶ *Using the AT commands*
▶ *Understanding your modem's status lights*
▶ *Calling a remote system*
▶ *Sign-on procedures*

Now that everything's hooked up and ready to go, you're probably anxious to make that initial call and take the first step down the road to connecting your PC to other computers. Don't worry, that's exactly what we'll do, a little later in this chapter. On the way from here to there, however, there are still a few basic items to cover.

The AT Command Set

As mentioned in the previous two chapters, most PC modems support the AT command set. This command set was introduced by Hayes Microcomputer Products, Inc., the first company to introduce "smart modems" (i.e., modems capable of being reprogrammed by software commands) to the PC marketplace. Due to the ensuing popularity of the Hayes modem line, its internal command structure (the AT command set) quickly became the standard for PC communications. Today, virtually every modem manufacturer strives to make their products *Hayes-compatible* (i.e., they recognize and respond to the AT command set).

What Are AT Commands?

The AT command set derives its name from the fact that the letters *AT* (special code to get the modem's ATtention) precede instructions sent to a modem from your PC. For example, the AT command that tells a modem to dial a number using the touch-tone method is ATDT (ATtention Dial Tone). Conversely, you would use ATDP (ATtention Dial Pulse) to place your calls on a phone system that does not support touch-tone dialing. Many AT commands are mnemonic in nature, meaning the command itself reflects the operation being performed.

Other mnemonic AT commands include:

▶ *ATA (ATtention Answer)*. Used to force a modem to answer an incoming call, even if it's not set for the Auto-Answer mode.
▶ *ATB (ATtention Bell protocol)*. Used to specify handshake options, using standard Bell protocols.
▶ *ATE (ATtention Echo)*. Used to turn the local echo of characters during an on-line session on and off.
▶ *ATH (ATtention Hangup)*. Used to connect or disconnect a modem from the phone line.
▶ *ATO (ATtention return On-line)*. Used to return a modem to on-line status following command execution.

If all AT commands were this straightforward and easy to memorize, telecommunications would be a simple proposition, indeed. You would issue an easy command, your modem would respond, and that would be the end of it. Unfortunately, this is not the case. To prove my point, let's take a look at some other AT commands that aren't so obvious:

▶ *ATZ*. Used to reconfigure a modem to its default settings.
▶ *ATV*. Used to specify whether a modem will display the results of specific operations such as a numeric code or text message.

► *ATM*. Used to specify when a modem's speaker is active. Common choices are: never, only until a connection is established, or always.

► *ATL*. Used to internally set a modem's speaker volume; some modems have an external knob, similar to the volume control on a tape player, that serves this same function.

In addition, there is the AT Set register command (ATS), a single command that modifies several modem settings, depending on the value that follows it. For example:

► *ATS0*. Used to specify how many times the phone will ring before your modem answers the line, when set to the Auto-Answer mode.

► *ATS8*. Used to specify how long your modem will pause whenever it encounters a comma in a dial string.

► *ATS9*. Used to set how long your modem will wait to terminate a call, if it does not reach a modem on the other end.

► *ATS10*. Used to set how long your modem will wait after the other computer drops its signal before hanging up the line on your end.

67

Cutting Through the Clutter

While the AT command set superimposed a standard over the previously chaotic field of modem communications, using it is not an activity to be undertaken by the passive beginner or faint of heart. So, must you become an expert at using the AT command set to telecommunicate? Fortunately, no. Most communications programs alleviate the intimidation associated with telecommunications by positioning themselves between you and the AT command set.

As a rule, for example, you don't need to know that ATE1 is the AT command to switch from half- to full-duplex; that is, to specify whether the characters you type will immediately appear on your display, or be echoed back across the phone line after they are received by the other computer. All you have to be familiar with is the procedure your communications program uses to toggle between Echo On (full-duplex) and Echo Off (half-duplex). In Procomm Plus, for example, this is accomplished with an Alt-E (Echo) keystroke. Other communications programs may use a different key combination or procedure, but the underlying principle is the same.

Using AT Commands

There may be times, however, when it's more efficient to use the AT commands. Suppose, for example, that you're getting ready to connect with a remote system that you never called before and, chances are, you'll never call again. In such a case, it would be simpler to place the call directly from your communications software's terminal screen, using the appropriate AT Dial command. Otherwise, you would have to go through all the steps required to include information on that system's connect procedures and communications parameters in a Dialing Directory, which is a feature common to many communications programs that allows you to automate contacting remote systems that you call on a regular basis.

To allow this, most communications programs include a *Terminal Mode* option, where any instructions you type in are immediately sent to the modem, rather than translated from the software's commands or menu options into a corresponding AT command.

To see how this is done, we're going to use the AT Dial command to have your modem call . . . well . . . yourself.

Dialing Direct

To begin with, if your communications program is not already running, go ahead and load it now. Also, be sure to turn your modem on. For this exercise, you won't have to worry about either the program or modem settings.

> ► **Note:** Many communications programs immediately take you to the Terminal mode, where the commands you type in transmit directly to your modem. You must be in the Terminal mode for AT commands to execute successfully. If this is not the case, check your documentation. (Suggestion: Look in the index under "Terminal Mode.") If necessary, use the appropriate command to switch your program to the Terminal mode.

Are you ready? Good. Because it's time to make your first modem connection.

▶ *To enter the AT Dial command on a touch-tone line:*

Type   ATDT

Press   *Spacebar*

▶ *To enter the AT Dial command if your telephone system still uses pulse dialing:*

Type   ATDP

Press   *Spacebar*

Type   *your telephone number, in the format* ###-#### (where each # represents a digit of your phone number).

Press   *Enter*

Depending on the type of modem you have, and how that modem and your communications program are configured, one or more of the following should have happened:

69

▶ If your modem has a speaker, and that speaker is set to remain on at least until *carrier detect* (when a connection is established), then you would have heard a dial tone followed by the sounds of the modem dialing your number. (On a touch-tone line, this last item would have been audible tones. However, with pulse dialing, you would have heard a series of clicks.)

▶ If your modem is set to return text messages (remember this from the ATV command mentioned previously), then the word BUSY appeared on your screen (after all, you were calling your own phone line), and the modem automatically dropped the line.

▶ If your modem does not automatically determine line status, then you saw no message and your modem is still connected, vainly trying to complete the call.

The Hangup Command

Of course, you probably don't want to leave your modem just sitting there, listening to an incessant busy signal. The good news is, you don't have to. The AT Hangup command lets you quickly disconnect your modem from a remote system.

▶ *To disconnect the current connection:*

Type   +++ ATH0

Press   *Enter*

> ▶ **Note:** If for some reason the AT Hangup command does not disconnect your call, you can accomplish the same thing by turning off your modem and then turning it back on again. Although this procedure should only be used as a last resort, go ahead and do it now, if necessary.

Congratulations! You just attempted your first communications session with your modem. Never mind that you only called yourself and reached a busy signal. The important thing is that you did it. Now let's talk a little bit about what you did.

Specifically, you:

1. Entered the ATDx command, where x was either a T or a P, depending on the type of phone system you were using.
2. Pressed the Spacebar to insert a space after the AT Dial command.
3. Typed in your telephone number.
4. Pressed Enter to transmit the preceding command sequence to your modem.
5. Used the standard AT Escape sequence (+++) to temporarily interrupt the current session and alert your modem that another AT command was coming.
6. Used the ATH0 command to disconnect the current call.

To be honest, the space you put between the ATDx command and your phone number was optional. Any modem that's fully Hayes-compatible recognizes an AT Dial command entered in several formats, including:

▶ ATDT#######
▶ ATDT###-####
▶ ATDT #######
▶ ATDT ####-####

Similarly, valid formats for long-distance calls include:

▶ ATDT1#########
▶ ATDT1-###-###-####
▶ ATDT1(###)###-####
▶ ATDT 1 ### ### ####
▶ ATDT 1-###-###-####
▶ ATDT 1 (###) ###-####

Basically, modems ignore any nonnumeric characters (spaces, dashes, brackets, etc.) included in phone numbers that follow an ATDx command. (One important exception to this rule is the comma, which we'll discuss shortly.) Personally, I find that entering the numbers I'm dialing in a familiar format such as ###-#### helps organize my befuddled mind.

71

The AT Redial Command

Now that you've seen how to use the AT Dial and Hangup commands, let's try one more exercise before moving on. Specifically, one in which you will use the AT Redial command to call yourself a second time.

 To retry the previous call:
Type   A/

A/, another member of the Hayes AT command family, lets you automatically redial the last number called. (Of course, the previous chain of events merely repeated themselves—possibly including the need to manually disconnect the call with an ATH0 Hangup command or by turning your modem off and then back on again. If this is the case, go ahead and do so now.)

As stated earlier in this section, it is rare to have to issue AT commands directly. Most of the time, your communications program's own command structure initiates on-line activities. In turn, it converts your requests to the appropriate AT command. Still, it's good to understand something about what the AT commands do and how to use them, should the need ever arise.

Lights, Modem, Action

If you use an external modem, you can tell a lot about what's happening during a communications session simply by watching its status lights. As a rule, these status lights are located across an external modem's front panel, as illustrated in Figure 5.1. Whenever you make a remote connection, these lights turn off and on to show the status of a number of communications parameters or modem operations. This information can be extremely helpful if you're having problems making a connection, installing your modem or communications software, or setting up a new on-line service. (Remember, an internal modem is hidden inside the PC cabinet. Consequently, including status lights in their design would be superfluous. Sorry, internal modem owners, you'll just have to set a string of miniature Christmas tree lights near your PC if you want a comparable display during your on-line sessions.)

72

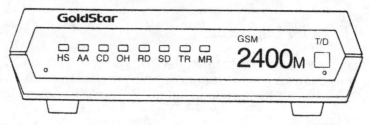

Figure 5.1 The status lights on an external modem reveal information about its operations.

The exact location of a modem's status lights and the order in which they appear varies from modem to modem. However, each light is usually labeled with a two-character abbreviation, indicating its function. Conditions revealed by a modem's status lights include:

▶ *MR (Modem Ready).* The MR light lets you know that your modem is turned on and ready to operate. If this indicator does not light up when you turn on your modem, check the connections for your power adapter. Make sure it is inserted securely into both the wall outlet and the back of your modem. If the problem persists, and you're certain the wall outlet works, you may need to replace your power adapter or possibly the whole modem.

► *RD (Receive Data)*. The RD light flickers each time the modem transfers data to your computer. This happens whenever your PC receives information of some kind from the remote system.

► *SD (Send Data)*. The SD light flickers each time your computer transfers data to the modem. This happens whenever you transmit information from your PC to the remote system.

► *AA (Auto Answer)*. The AA light goes on whenever your modem is set to the Auto-Answer mode, thus allowing your modem to automatically answer any incoming calls.

► *CD (Carrier Detect)*. The CD light goes on whenever your modem makes a connection with (or detects a carrier signal from) a remote computer. It should remain on for your entire on-line session. At the end of each call, one of the other computers disconnects its line, at which time the carrier signal is dropped and the CD light goes out.

► *OH (Off-Hook)*. The OH light goes on whenever your modem takes control of the phone line. This is equivalent to taking your telephone receiver off the hook. Hence, its name.

73

► *HS (High Speed)*. The HS light indicates that your modem is currently operating at its highest available transmission rate. Remember, most modems can communicate at multiple transmission rates (such as 300 bps, 1200 bps, 2400 bps, etc.). The HS indicator lets you tell (at a glance) if your modem is running at full speed.

► *TR (Terminal Ready)*. The TR light goes on when the modem detects a DTR (Data Terminal Ready) signal from your communications software. This signal informs your modem that a communications program is loaded and ready to run.

Knowing the function of each of these lights can be useful, should you experience problems during an on-line session. For example, if the RD light does not flicker during an unsuccessful file transfer, chances are the other computer system stopped sending data, and the transfer is either over, or it has failed. If, on the other hand, you're sending a file to another computer and the SD light stops flickering, that means your computer has stopped sending data.

Calling a Remote System

You now have a basic understanding of how the AT commands work. You also have an understanding of what your modem's status lights indicate and how they allow you, to some degree, to analyze whether and how well your modem is responding to specific on-line activities. Five chapters into your examination of modem communications and it's finally time to make your first official connection to a legitimate remote system, one that offers a variety of on-line options.

Which System?

One recurring problem an author faces when putting together a book on modem communications is how to provide concrete, interactive examples of what the reader can expect to see, once he or she finally has everything up and running and is ready to telecommunicate. Theoretical discussions and objective descriptions can only accomplish so much. To truly learn what telecommunications is all about, nothing can replace the experience of dialing a legitimate on-line service and seeing, first hand, what happens.

However, which system should you call? Commercial on-line services like CompuServe, Prodigy, DELPHI, and GEnie restrict access to paid subscribers. (Don't believe for a minute, however, that I plan to ignore these services. Subsequent chapters contain concrete examples of what they offer and how they work. Additionally, you'll find information on how to subscribe to some of the more popular commercial on-line services in Appendix A.) A local *bulletin board system (BBS)*, on the other hand, though generally open to the public, simply isn't set up to handle the number of calls that could result from its inclusion in a book that is bought by thousands of individuals who could potentially contact that BBS to perform the hands-on tasks it contains.

As a result of my extensive experience in modem communications, I'm intimately familiar with this dilemma. I'm also lucky to have developed contacts to help me pull a few strings and come up with a workable solution to this problem. Before continuing, therefore, I'd like to thank Vulcan Publications and Doug Kilarski, the Editor-in-Chief of "Vulcan's Computer Monthly" for permitting me to use their on-line service, the *Computer Monthly Electronic Edition (CMEE)*, for the following exercises. Because of them, I can provide examples of using your modem to access a remote system. Thanks, fellas.

> ▶ **Note:** One thing even I can't manage is to convince telephone companies like AT&T or Sprint to suspend the long-distance charges incurred when calling CMEE. Consequently, be prepared to see a small increase in your phone bill for the time you spend on-line performing the following exercises. Don't panic, though. Wherever possible, I've structured your on-line activities to keep this time to a minimum. Still, long-distance charges and access fees are an unavoidable fact of life for anyone who telecommunicates with any regularity.

CMEE provides a variety of on-line services, including a hardware and software buyer's guide. This guide is a convenient way for readers of "Vulcan's Computer Monthly" to submit suggestions, comments, and questions, to the magazine's editors and writers. CMEE also contains special areas for downloading and uploading files to and from the system. Before accessing any of these features, however, you must use your modem to call CMEE and register with the system. As is true of most on-line services, this involves providing some basic information about yourself and then defining the procedures CMEE will use to recognize you in the future.

Getting Ready

It's time to start applying some of that technical information we've been discussing over the past four chapters, so stay with me.

To begin with, CMEE uses the following communications parameters:

Baud:	1200, 2400, or 9600 bps
Parity:	None
Data bits:	8
Stop bits:	1
Duplex:	Full

Before calling CMEE, therefore, configure your modem to match these settings, using the appropriate procedures for your communications software. With Procomm Plus, for example, you accomplish this by entering an Alt-P (Parameters) command and then specifying the desired settings at the subsequent prompt screen. Other programs may use a different command to modify their settings.

As the above listing illustrates, CMEE handles modem calls placed at either 1200 or 2400 baud, the two most popular baud rates currently used for PC communications. (Additionally, the 1200-baud access line can accommodate 9600-baud connections.) The one you need depends on the maximum baud rate your modem supports.

Placing the Call

Once your software is configured properly, you're ready to make that initial registration call. In this first exercise, we'll use the AT Dial command to access the appropriate CMEE number for your modem's baud rate. The specific command you enter depends on which baud rate you select and whether your local phone system supports touch-tone or pulse dialing.

> ▶ **Note:** If you live in or around Birmingham, Alabama, the corporate headquarters of Vulcan Publications, Inc., contacting CMEE may be a local call. If you don't normally include an area code when dialing that city, delete the "1-205-" portion of the following AT Dial commands.

▶ *If you own a 1200- or 9600-baud modem and your telephone system supports touch-tone dialing:*

Type   `ATDT 1-205-655-4065`
Press   *Enter*

▶ *If you own a 1200- or 9600-baud modem and your telephone system requires pulse dialing:*

Type   `ATDP 1-205-655-4065`
Press   *Enter*

▶ *If you own a 2400-baud modem and your telephone system supports touch-tone dialing:*

Type   `ATDT 1-205-655-4059`
Press   *Enter*

▶ *If you own a 2400-baud modem and your telephone system requires pulse dialing:*

Type   `ATDP 1-205-655-4059`
Press   *Enter*

Your modem dials the number you specify to contact CMEE at the appropriate baud rate. If a line is available (i.e., if you do not encounter a busy signal) CMEE automatically accepts your call and, after a few seconds, displays the welcome message shown in Figure 5.2. Although it appears on your display, this message is being sent over the phone line by CMEE.

You just made your first successful on-line connection to another computer. That wasn't too difficult, was it?

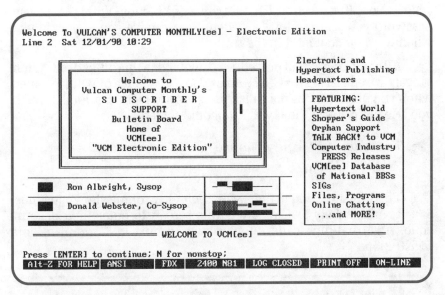

Figure 5.2 Whenever anyone calls CMEE, it displays its opening Welcome screen.

Now that you're connected to CMEE, why not register with it?

> **Note:** Some modems or computers require that you press Enter once a connection is made, to wake up the remote system. If you hear something that sounds like static (the sound of two modems trying to establish a connection with one another), followed by silence, and then nothing appears on your display, press Enter once or twice to alert CMEE to your presence.

A Typical Registration Sequence

Like most commercial on-line services and BBSs, CMEE requires you to provide it with some basic information before granting access to all of its features. This is done for your own protection and for the protection of the service or BBS. If someone misuses a system, for example, its system operator (or sysop) would be able to identify that individual and take the appropriate steps to prevent him or her from doing so again. Conversely, registering for a system allows you to specify an *account code* (also called a *user ID*) that, in conjunction with the private password you select, allows a system to recognize you as a valid user whenever you contact it in the future.

Although the actual procedures involved in this differ from system to system, registering for CMEE gives you a good idea of what to expect when you place your initial call to many on-line services. First, though, you need to get past the CMEE Welcome screen.

78

▶ *To continue to the next phase of CMEE registration:*
Press   *Enter*

This advances you to the CMEE Sign-On prompt, shown in Figure 5.3. Regular callers to CMEE use this screen to enter their account code. As a first-time caller, however, you must first complete your registration.

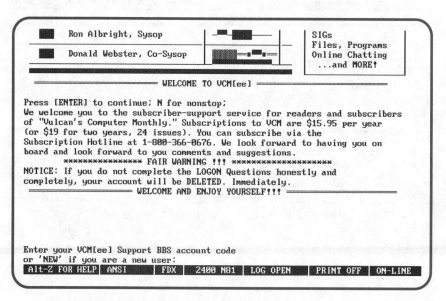

Figure 5.3 The CMEE Sign-On prompt.

▶ *To register as a new user to CMEE:*

Type   NEW

Press   *Enter*

This advances you to the prompt shown in Figure 5.4. This prompt asks you to enter your account code, the first piece of information it requires to process your registration.

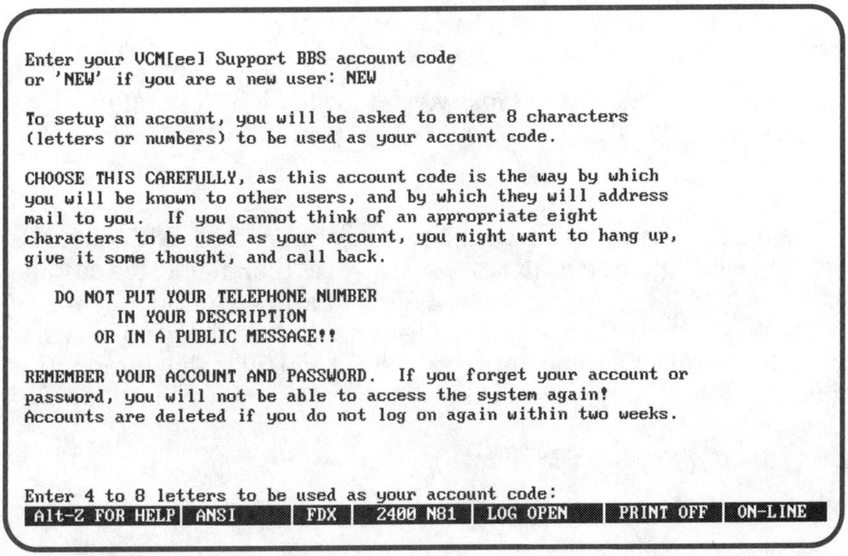

```
Enter your VCM[ee] Support BBS account code
or 'NEW' if you are a new user: NEW

To setup an account, you will be asked to enter 8 characters
(letters or numbers) to be used as your account code.

CHOOSE THIS CAREFULLY, as this account code is the way by which
you will be known to other users, and by which they will address
mail to you.  If you cannot think of an appropriate eight
characters to be used as your account, you might want to hang up,
give it some thought, and call back.

    DO NOT PUT YOUR TELEPHONE NUMBER
         IN YOUR DESCRIPTION
         OR IN A PUBLIC MESSAGE!!

REMEMBER YOUR ACCOUNT AND PASSWORD.  If you forget your account or
password, you will not be able to access the system again!
Accounts are deleted if you do not log on again within two weeks.



Enter 4 to 8 letters to be used as your account code:
Alt-Z FOR HELP| ANSI     | FDX  | 2400 N81 | LOG OPEN  | PRINT OFF | ON-LINE
```

79

Figure 5.4 As a new user, you must provide CMEE with certain preliminary information to enter the system.

Your user ID is the unique name assigned to your account. It is also the name other callers will use to identify you on this system. It should, therefore, be something easy to remember. One common approach people take is to select some variation of their name. In the exercises that follow, for example, I'll use JACKN.

▶ *To specify your CMEE account code:*

Type   *a user ID* (four to eight letters in length)

Press   *Enter*

At this point, CMEE displays a prompt asking you to input a password to assign to your account code. Unlike your user ID, your password should be somewhat cryptic in nature. Passwords guard against unauthorized callers accessing your account on a system, many of which charge for connect time. Therefore, select a password that is not obvious, but can be easily remembered. I don't want to instill paranoia, but anyone who knows your user ID and password can access your account on a remote computer, appearing like you whenever they sign on to that system. Thus, I recommend using an obscure password. Avoid including a variation of your name, home town, spouse's name, or anything equally obvious, in your passwords. Also, it's a good idea to select a different password on each remote system for which you are registered—again, for security's sake.

 To specify your CMEE password:

Type	*appropriate password* (four to eight letters in length)
Press	*Enter*

After recording your account code and password, CMEE requests additional information from new users such as their name, the city and state in which they live, and a short, three-line description they would like associated with their account. The prompts associated with each of these items are self-explanatory, so go ahead and fill in that information now.

80

 To complete your CMEE registration:

Type	*your full name*
Press	*Enter*
Type	*the city and state in which you live*
Press	*Enter*
Type	*an optional description of yourself.*

> **Note:** Your personal description can be up to three lines in length. This is the information CMEE displays, along with your full name and location, to other users who request information about you, based on your account code. Most on-line services provide some means for callers to get to know other registered users. A little later on, CMEE will request additional information about you, which is accessible only to the system operator.

Once you have entered this preliminary information, CMEE requests that you reenter your account code and password. Although the system displays your account code as you enter it, you can't see it. A series of asterisks (*) is substituted for your password, as shown in Figure 5.5. This is done for security purposes, so others cannot see your password during the normal sign-on procedure.

You are now officially signed on to CMEE. At this point, you should see a screen resembling Figure 5.5. The specific announcements on your screen, which are regularly updated by system operator Dr. Ron Albright, will differ from the ones shown here.

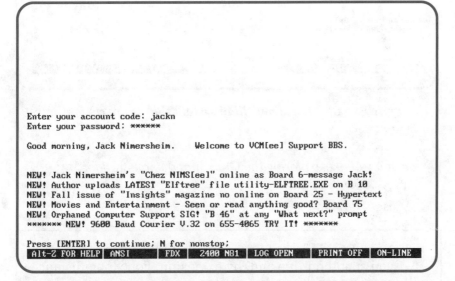

```
Enter your account code: jackn
Enter your password: ******

Good morning, Jack Nimersheim.    Welcome to VCM[ee] Support BBS.

NEW! Jack Nimersheim's "Chez NIMS[ee]" online as Board 6-message Jack!
NEW! Author uploads LATEST "Elftree" file utility-ELFTREE.EXE on B 10
NEW! Fall issue of "Insights" magazine no online on Board 25 - Hypertext
NEW! Movies and Entertainment - Seen or read anything good? Board 75
NEW! Orphaned Computer Support SIG! "B 46" at any "What next?" prompt
******* NEW! 9600 Baud Courier V.32 on 655-4065 TRY IT! *******

Press [ENTER] to continue; N for nonstop;
Alt-Z FOR HELP  ANSI      FDX   2400 N81  LOG OPEN   PRINT OFF  ON-LINE
```

Figure 5.5 After requesting your account code and password a second time, CMEE grants you access to the system.

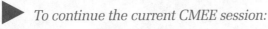 *To continue the current CMEE session:*
Press   *Enter*

CMEE is a multiline system, meaning more than one caller can access it at any given time. Whenever you call CMEE, it displays a listing of any users currently on-line, including yourself, as shown in Figure 5.6. (CMEE includes a Chat feature that allows you to communicate directly with other callers included in this list.) Since this is your first time on the system, CMEE also asks if you're interested in seeing a demonstration of its bulletin board software, the Oracomm BBS.

```
Enter your account code: jackn
Enter your password: ******

Good morning, Jack Nimersheim.    Welcome to VCM[ee] Support BBS.


NEW! Jack Nimersheim's "Chez NIMS[ee]" online as Board 6-message Jack!
NEW! Author uploads LATEST "Elftree" file utility-ELFTREE.EXE on B 10
NEW! Fall issue of "Insights" magazine no online on Board 25 - Hypertext
NEW! Movies and Entertainment - Seen or read anything good? Board 75
NEW! Orphaned Computer Support SIG! "B 46" at any "What next?" prompt
******* NEW! 9600 Baud Courier V.32 on 655-4065 TRY IT! *******

Press [ENTER] to continue; N for nonstop;

You can be online 59 minutes this session.


Users Currently Online
  Line Account  Cmnd
    1  SANLY
    2  JACKN
Do you want a demonstration of how to use this BBS ([Y]/N)?
Alt-Z FOR HELP| ANSI  |  FDX  | 2400 N81 | LOG OPEN |  PRINT OFF | ON-LINE
```

82

Figure 5.6 CMEE is a multiline system that supports multiple callers.

▶ *If you feel like exploring the Oracomm demonstration:*
Type   Y
Press   *Enter*

▶ **Note:** Keep in mind, however, that this extends the time you spend on-line and, by extension, your long-distance bill increases for this initial session.

▶ *To bypass this demonstration:*
Type   N
Press   *Enter*

As mentioned earlier, CMEE requests additional, private information from first-time users, as shown in Figure 5.7. The information you enter during this sequence can only be accessed by authorized system operators—specifically, Dr. Albright and his colleague, Donald Webster, the two gentlemen responsible for coordinating CMEE. Information you enter here includes:

▶ your real name
▶ your area code and telephone number
▶ your street address
▶ your city, state, and zip code

That's the full extent of the personal information CMEE requests, certainly no more than any legitimate caller would feel comfortable supplying.

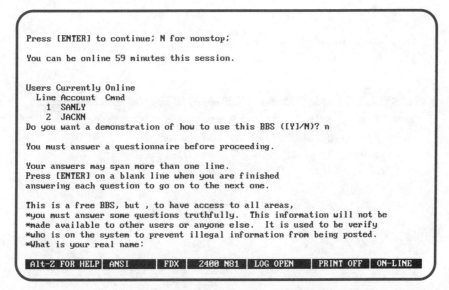

```
Press [ENTER] to continue; N for nonstop;

You can be online 59 minutes this session.


Users Currently Online
  Line Account  Cmnd
    1  SANLY
    2  JACKN
Do you want a demonstration of how to use this BBS ([Y]/N)? n

You must answer a questionnaire before proceeding.

Your answers may span more than one line.
Press [ENTER] on a blank line when you are finished
answering each question to go on to the next one.

This is a free BBS, but , to have access to all areas,
*you must answer some questions truthfully.  This information will not be
*made available to other users or anyone else.  It is used to be verify
*who is on the system to prevent illegal information from being posted.
*What is your real name:

 Alt-Z FOR HELP| ANSI    |   FDX  | 2400 N81 | LOG OPEN  | PRINT OFF | ON-LINE
```

83

Figure 5.7 Most commercial services and BBSs, including CMEE, request additional information from new users the first time they call.

After entering your personal information, you see the cryptic prompt shown at the bottom of Figure 5.8. Don't let this intimidate you. The one complaint I have with the Oracomm software is its tendency to present ambiguous prompts. Notice, however, that one of these is a question mark (?), which you can use whenever it's displayed to request additional information about the current prompt. Most commercial information services and local BBSs include a similar Help feature (on-line help from an on-line service), although the method used to access it differs from system to system. For now, however, all you want to do is record your registration information, using the SAVE (S) command, and then move on.

```
Press [ENTER] on a blank line when you are finished
answering each question to go on to the next one.

This is a free BBS, but , to have access to all areas,
*you must answer some questions truthfully.  This information will not be
*made available to other users or anyone else.  It is used to be verify
*who is on the system to prevent illegal information from being posted.
*What is your real name:
Jack Nimersheim


What is your area code and telephone number:
(812) 427-2614


What is your mailing street addres: 306 East Main Street


What is your mailing city, state, zipcode:
Vevay, IN 47043



Enter  I999,R999,D999,E999,L,S,C or ?
 Alt-Z FOR HELP   ANSI     FDX    2400 N81   LOG OPEN    PRINT OFF   ON-LINE
```

Figure 5.8 Although its options are sometimes confusing, CMEE provides a Help command (?) to request additional information about an on-line activity or command.

▶ *To record your registration information with CMEE:*

Type   S

Press   *Enter*

Ending Your First Session

Again, congratulations! You are now a registered user of CMEE, and you can call back at any time without having to reenter the information supplied in the previous exercises. From now on, after supplying your account code and password, you'll be taken almost immediately to the system's main menu, shown in Figure 5.9, from which you can select what you want to do on-line from a wide range of options. We'll be looking at how some of these options work in subsequent exercises in this book. For now, let's use the the QUICK Log-Off option to end this initial CMEE session, go off-line, and return to your communications program.

▶ *To end this initial CMEE session:*
Type   Q
Press   *Enter*

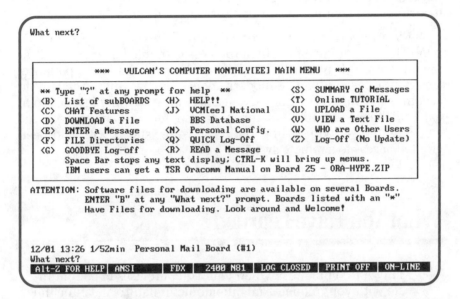

```
What next?

┌─────────────────────────────────────────────────────────────────┐
│        ***   VULCAN'S COMPUTER MONTHLY[EE] MAIN MENU   ***         │
│                                                                   │
│  ** Type "?" at any prompt for help  **      <S>  SUMMARY of Messages │
│  <B>  List of subBOARDS    <H>  HELP!!       <T>  Online TUTORIAL  │
│  <C>  CHAT Features        <J>  VCM[ee] National <U>  UPLOAD a File │
│  <D>  DOWNLOAD a File           BBS Database  <V>  VIEW a Text File │
│  <E>  ENTER a Message      <N>  Personal Config. <W>  WHO are Other Users │
│  <F>  FILE Directories     <Q>  QUICK Log-Off <Z>  Log-Off (No Update) │
│  <G>  GOODBYE Log-off      <R>  READ a Message │
│       Space Bar stops any text display; CTRL-K will bring up menus. │
│       IBM users can get a TSR Oracomm Manual on Board 25 - ORA-HYPE.ZIP │
├─────────────────────────────────────────────────────────────────┤
│  ATTENTION: Software files for downloading are available on several Boards. │
│             ENTER "B" at any "What next?" prompt. Boards listed with an "*" │
│             Have Files for downloading. Look around and Welcome! │

   12/01 13:26 1/52min  Personal Mail Board (#1)
   What next?
   Alt-Z FOR HELP  ANSI  │  FDX  │  2400 N81  │  LOG CLOSED  │  PRINT OFF  │  ON-LINE
```

Figure 5.9 Like many remote systems, CMEE uses a main menu to list its various on-line options.

85

Sign on and then sign right off again. It seems kind of unproductive, doesn't it? Not really. You actually accomplished quite a bit on this initial call:

▶ First, you learned how to contact a remote system with your modem and communications program.

▶ Second, you got a general idea of the procedures used to sign on to a remote system.

▶ Third, you registered yourself as an authorized user with CMEE. Consequently, whenever you place another call to this particular system (which we'll do in the next chapter), you'll be taken almost immediately to its main menu.

▶ Finally, you learned how to end an on-line session, using the Oracomm QUICK Log-Off command.

Not bad for a few minutes of your time and a few pennies in long-distance telephone charges, I'd say. Furthermore, although the specific commands used to accomplish something vary from system to system, the general procedures outlined in the previous exercises are common to virtually all commercial on-line services and BBSs.

Most importantly, however, you have dipped your toes into the pool of telecommunications. In the process, it should have become clear to you that this is not really some mysterious or mystical experience. You simply used a pair of modern tools; your PC and a modem, to accomplish some very impressive feats. And we've only just begun to explore the possibilities. In the next chapter we'll examine some amazing things to do on-line, once you've registered with and been granted access to a remote system.

What You Have Learned

▶ Many AT commands, which your software uses to communicate with your modem, are mnemonic in nature, meaning the command itself reflects the operation being performed.

▶ External modems include several status lights used to show the current conditions of a variety of communications parameters and modem operations. This information can be extremely useful if you're having problems making a connection, installing your modem or communications software, or setting up a new on-line service.

▶ Although minor differences do exist, many commercial services and BBSs use similar procedures to grant access to callers. As a rule, most remote systems require you to supply specific information about yourself the first time you call, including a user ID (or account code) and password, so you can be registered and recognized as a valid user from that point on.

Chapter 6

Logged On and Ready To Go

In This Chapter

▶ *Electronic messaging*
▶ *Participating in a real-time conference*

Now that you've dipped your toes into the warm waters of telecommunications, it's time to take the plunge. You are about to dive into the deep end of two very popular on-line activities: sending and receiving electronic mail and participating in real-time conferences.

Electronic Messaging

As I pointed out in Chapter 1, it's estimated that 8 to 15 million people currently rely on electronic messaging for at least a portion of their regular correspondence. And why not? Exchanging information with a computer can be fast, reliable, convenient, and potentially less expensive than regular mail.

One of the main reasons why many people use their PC to connect with other computers is *electronic messaging* (also called *electronic mail* or *E-mail*). E-mail combines the convenience of a telephone call with the reliability of traditional postal delivery to provide the perfect communication mechanism for busy individuals caught up in the frenetic pace of life in the late 20th century.

E-mail allows you to compose and transmit a message whenever it is convenient for you, just as the telephone allows you to pick it up and dial when your schedule permits. You can then post your electronic message to an on-line service immediately, regardless of where the person to whom it is being sent may be, or what he or she is doing at the time.

Electronic messaging differs from a traditional phone call in that, in order for the latter to succeed, the sending and receiving party must be available at the same time. Whereas, people receiving electronic messages retrieve them at their convenience. Consequently, neither party's important work is interrupted and correspondence still flows reliably and with relative speed. In fact, electronic messaging is so convenient it's almost addicting. I check my various on-line services at least twice a day. Anyone who communicates with me using E-mail, therefore, can rest assured that there's never more than a twelve-hour delay in my getting their important messages. Should a particularly crucial item require a faster turnaround time than this, they always have the old-fashioned telephone to fall back on.

Another appealing factor of electronic messaging is the increasing movement toward a global village. While you're working hard at your desk here in the United States, individuals in the European markets might have already punched out their time cards and called it a day. If so, arranging a telephone conference with an international co-worker would be difficult, at best. Would you drag yourself into the office at five in the morning? Or could your co-worker hang on past his normal 5 p.m. quitting time? E-mail eliminates this dilemma. The computer relaying your messages through an on-line service doesn't care what time it is in Boston, Berlin, New York, or Newcastle. Barring a system crash, that computer remains at your beck and call twenty-four hours a day, seven days a week, and doesn't even complain about being overworked and underpaid.

As an added attraction, communicating over E-mail can be less expensive than a regular phone call. For example, transmitting a three- or four-page letter over CompuServe's Mail service sets me back me about 42¢. Can you imagine how much it would cost to convey the same amount of information, if "Ma Bell" or some other long-distance carrier were tallying up the charges for an overseas connection?

Because of its increased convenience and decreased costs, E-mail obviously has a lot going for it—at least enough to warrant its consideration as a practical alternative to your current communication methods. However, if this consideration evolves into an actual commitment, what options do you have? I'm glad you asked.

On-Line Options

No one recognizes the potential of electronic messaging more than the various companies who provide it. They've jumped on the E-mail bandwagon "faster than fleas on a beagle" (as my father would say). Virtually every commercial information service includes electronic messaging in their on-line offerings. On CompuServe, as I've already pointed out, you send and receive E-mail by accessing its Mail function. On DELPHI and BIX, a MAIL command serves similar yeoman's duty. Other commercial services offer comparable functions.

In addition to being one of many options offered by commerical on-line services, electronic messaging represents the exclusive product of several dedicated E-mail services. A partial listing of these services includes:

- ▶ AT&T Mail
- ▶ Sprint Mail
- ▶ Western Union Easylink

Astute readers immediately recognize the obvious thread running through this listing. Traditional phone companies—or, in the case of Western Union, a company that originally found its fortune in the now-outmoded field of telegraphy—have taken to E-mail like ducks to water. They have recognized the inherent advantages of electronic messaging over standard telephone communications and have no desire to be left out in the cold when the next wave of E-mail subscribers arrives. Besides, they're natural candidates to provide electronic messaging. After all, these companies already have a nationwide—and, in fact, an international—communications network, a prerequisite to efficiently disseminating electronic messages on a large scale.

Although the specific procedures employed to pass electronic messages back and forth vary for each service (whether it is a dedicated E-mail provider or one of the more diverse commercial services) the overall process is standard. You enter the appropriate command for the service you choose to use, identify who will receive the current message, optionally enter a short description of its contents, write the message, and then send it on its way.

The next time the intended recipient signs on to that service, whether it be two minutes or two months later, he or she will see some type of notice indicating that they have E-mail waiting for them. (Most commercial services display this notice immediately or, at least, within a few minutes. If the recipient is on-line at the time, the service discreetly interrupts to achieve the same reliable delivery.)

The fact that the above scenario bears a striking resemblance to the steps normally required to write and deliver a letter through the U.S. Postal Service is no accident. (They don't call this E-mail for nothing.) To give you an idea of what I mean, let's take a look at a typical E-mail transaction over CompuServe, arguably the most popular commercial on-line information service.

Why CompuServe?

By showcasing CompuServe here, I am not implying that it is the only on-line service worthy of handling your E-mail activities; I'm not even saying it's the best. It is, however, one of the most successful. With over 625,000 subscribers, CompuServe provides immediate access to more users than any other currently active commercial service. As an added attraction, the CompuServe Mail option transfers electronic messages to users of several other popular service, including MCI Mail (easily the most popular dedicated E-mail company). CompuServe also includes an option to transfer messages from its Mail area directly to any Group-III FAX machine. It even allows you to have printed copies of E-mail correspondence delivered as regular mail, should the intended recipient not possess E-mail capabilities. Finally, a large percentage of modems sold today ship with instructions on how to receive and, in some cases, discounts that can be applied to an introductory subscription to CompuServe. (If your modem did not include such an offer, check out Appendix A for information on how to contact CompuServe and inquire about becoming a subscriber.)

Sending E-Mail Over CompuServe

The first step in preparing to contact CompuServe is to match your modem's parameters to CompuServe's. The correct communications parameters for CompuServe are:

- ▶ 1200, 2400, or 9600 baud
- ▶ Even parity
- ▶ 7 data bits
- ▶ 1 stop bit
- ▶ Full duplex

Once your modem's settings match CompuServe's requirements, you're ready for contact, using the appropriate access number.

Identifying an Access Number

The telephone number you use to contact a remote system depends on several factors. In some cases, one or two access numbers are provided for all callers, regardless of who they are and where they are calling from. In the previous chapter, for example, you used one of two access numbers to contact the CMEE. Which of these two numbers you called depended strictly on the baud rate you used. As a rule, the one- or two-number access approach is used when you contact a corporate mainframe or local BBS from your PC.

91

More commonly, however, and especially when you make a connection to a nationwide commercial information service like CompuServe, the specific number you use depends on three factors:

- ▶ the method you use to access that remote system
- ▶ where you are calling from
- ▶ the baud rate at which you are communicating

Many commercial information services are accessed through a *packet-switching network*. Stated simply, a packet-switching network resembles a super switchboard, through which incoming calls to a single, *local access number* are routed to any one of several commercial services. After making a connection to the packet-switching network, you are asked to identify the service you're trying to call. The network, in turn, forwards your call to that service.

Providing access through a packet-switching network eliminates the need for each service to lease telephone lines in every major city from which people call—an expensive proposition. Instead, the individual commercial services that subscribe to a packet-switching network reduce their operating costs by each contributing a per-minute fee to that network. Two popular packet-switching networks are SprintNet and Tymnet, both of which are used to contact CompuServe.

The packet-switching network, in turn, assumes responsibility for maintaining local access numbers in a wide variety of locations. That's why the location you call from influences what number you call to access CompuServe. (Given CompuServe's popularity, however, that system possesses the financial resources to provide connect numbers in virtually every metropolitan area of the United States. Consequently, it's more convenient to bypass a packet-switching network and contact CompuServe directly. That's exactly what I'll do in the following sample exercise.)

Finally, packet-switching networks (and CompuServe) often provide separate numbers in various locations for different transmission rates. If this is the case where you live, then you would call a different number to make a 1200-baud connection, for example, than the one used to a 2400- or 9600-baud connection.

As a rule, when you subscribe to a commercial service, it will provide you with the appropriate access number, based on the three factors outlined above. Many even include a comprehensive listing of all their access numbers in the manual you receive as part of your subscription kit.

92

Contacting CompuServe Through SprintNet

Now that we've got that out of the way, let's go ahead and place a call to CompuServe. In the following exercise, I'll use the local CompuServe access number in Cincinnati, Ohio, for calls placed at 2400-baud. However, you'll need to substitute the correct access number for your location and transmission speed.

 To sign on to CompuServe using its 2400-baud Cincinnati number, I would:

Type   `ATDT 1-513-771-8543`

Press   *Enter*

> ▶ **Tip:** Here's where the advantages of a nationwide communications network come into play. If you don't know your local CompuServe access number, there's nothing to stop you from contacting that service through its Cincinnati number, shown above. Keep in mind, however, that doing so will add long-distance charges to your normal connect fees.

After a connection is made:

Press   *Enter to "wake up" CompuServe*

At the Host Name prompt:

Type   CIS

Press   *Enter*

At this point, your display should resemble Figure 6.1, which shows each of the previous steps being performed. The User ID prompt indicates that CompuServe is waiting for you to identify yourself, which it does by requesting your personal user ID and password. All commercial services use a similar sign-on procedure to verify that each caller is a valid subscriber and, by no small coincidence, to start the clock ticking for your per-minute access charges.

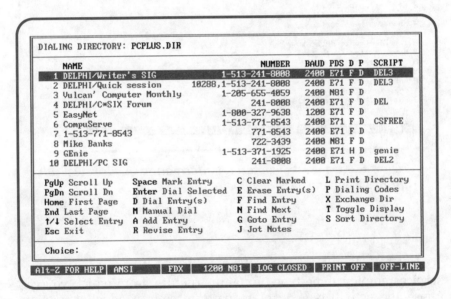

DIALING DIRECTORY: **PCPLUS.DIR**

	NAME	NUMBER	BAUD	PDS	D	P	SCRIPT
1	DELPHI/Writer's SIG	1-513-241-8008	2400	E71	F	D	DEL3
2	DELPHI/Quick session	10288,1-513-241-8008	2400	E71	F	D	DEL3
3	Vulcan' Computer Monthly	1-205-655-4059	2400	N81	F	D	
4	DELPHI/C*SIX Forum	241-8008	2400	E71	F	D	DEL
5	EasyNet	1-800-327-9638	1200	E71	F	D	
6	CompuServe	1-513-771-8543	2400	E71	F	D	CSFREE
7	1-513-771-8543	771-8543	2400	E71	F	D	
8	Mike Banks	722-3439	2400	N81	F	D	
9	GEnie	1-513-371-1925	2400	E71	H	D	genie
10	DELPHI/PC SIG	241-8008	2400	E71	F	D	DEL2

PgUp Scroll Up	**Space** Mark Entry	**C** Clear Marked	**L** Print Directory
PgDn Scroll Dn	**Enter** Dial Selected	**E** Erase Entry(s)	**P** Dialing Codes
Home First Page	**D** Dial Entry(s)	**F** Find Entry	**X** Exchange Dir
End Last Page	**M** Manual Dial	**N** Find Next	**T** Toggle Display
↑/↓ Select Entry	**A** Add Entry	**G** Goto Entry	**S** Sort Directory
Esc Exit	**R** Revise Entry	**J** Jot Notes	

Choice:

| Alt-Z FOR HELP | ANSI | FDX | 1200 N81 | LOG CLOSED | PRINT OFF | OFF-LINE |

Figure 6.1 A typical command sequence to sign on to CompuServe through one of its local access numbers.

▶ *To sign on to CompuServe:*

Type   *your user ID*

Press   *Enter*

At the Password prompt:

Type   *your password*

Press   *Enter*

If your user ID and password identifies you as a valid subscriber, you will advance to CompuServe's Main menu, shown in Figure 6.2.

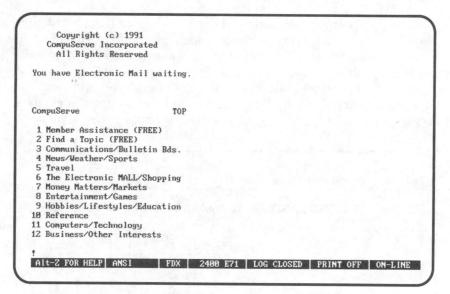

```
      Copyright (c) 1991
      CompuServe Incorporated
      All Rights Reserved

You have Electronic Mail waiting.
        ))


CompuServe                    TOP

   1 Member Assistance (FREE)
   2 Find a Topic (FREE)
   3 Communications/Bulletin Bds.
   4 News/Weather/Sports
   5 Travel
   6 The Electronic MALL/Shopping
   7 Money Matters/Markets
   8 Entertainment/Games
   9 Hobbies/Lifestyles/Education
  10 Reference
  11 Computers/Technology
  12 Business/Other Interests

 !
Alt-Z FOR HELP  ANSI    FDX   2400 E71  LOG CLOSED  PRINT OFF  ON-LINE
```

Figure 6.2 On most commercial information services you select options from an On-Screen menu.

Navigating CompuServe

As mentioned in the previous chapter, most commercial information services employ some type of menu structure, from which you can chose the activity you want to perform. As an added attraction, however, many services also provide command shortcuts for experienced users. Once you're familiar with a given service's command structure, using these shortcuts can considerably decrease the time spent on (and, by extension, the expense of) your on-line activities. In this case, I happen to know that the shortcut command to reach CompuServe Mail is GO MAIL. So, let's use it.

▶ *To access CompuServe Mail:*

Type   GO MAIL

Press   *Enter*

At this point, you are at the lowest level of this particular CompuServe option. Notice that you're no longer presented with an Option menu. Instead, CompuServe displays a simple input prompt associated with the Mail area, as shown in Figure 6.3.

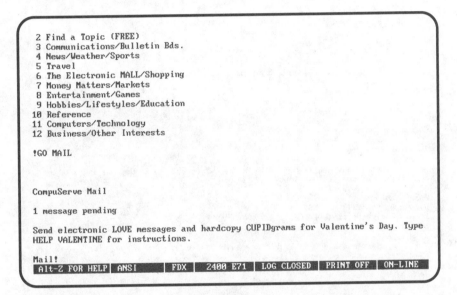

```
 2 Find a Topic (FREE)
 3 Communications/Bulletin Bds.
 4 News/Weather/Sports
 5 Travel
 6 The Electronic MALL/Shopping
 7 Money Matters/Markets
 8 Entertainment/Games
 9 Hobbies/Lifestyles/Education
10 Reference
11 Computers/Technology
12 Business/Other Interests

!GO MAIL



CompuServe Mail

1 message pending

Send electronic LOVE messages and hardcopy CUPIDgrams for Valentine's Day. Type
HELP VALENTINE for instructions.

Mail!
 Alt-Z FOR HELP │ ANSI     │  FDX  │ 2400 E71 │ LOG CLOSED │ PRINT OFF │ ON-LINE
```

Figure 6.3 At the lowest level of a command structure you may encounter a simple prompt associated with that facility.

Receiving Mail

Notice that as soon as I enter Mail, CompuServe informs me that I have one message waiting. (I already knew this. You'll see why in a few moments.) If this message did not appear, I would know my CompuServe mailbox was empty, and I could immediately back out of Mail.

▶ *To display the current message, I would:*

Type   READ

Press   *Enter*

95

The READ command causes CompuServe to display the Waiting message to my screen, as shown in Figure 6.4. Other commands available at the CompuServe Mail prompt include:

- ▶ SEND
- ▶ DELETE
- ▶ EXIT
- ▶ SAVE
- ▶ SCAN
- ▶ SEARCH
- ▶ HELP

96

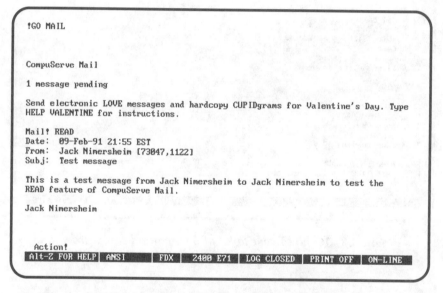

```
!GO MAIL


CompuServe Mail

1 message pending

Send electronic LOVE messages and hardcopy CUPIDgrams for Valentine's Day. Type
HELP VALENTINE for instructions.

Mail! READ
Date:   09-Feb-91 21:55 EST
From:   Jack Nimersheim [73047,1122]
Subj:   Test message

This is a test message from Jack Nimersheim to Jack Nimersheim to test the
READ feature of CompuServe Mail.

Jack Nimersheim



  Action!
 Alt-Z FOR HELP   ANSI       FDX    2400 E71   LOG CLOSED   PRINT OFF   ON-LINE
```

Figure 6.4 Pressing Enter automatically displays the message that was waiting in CompuServe Mail.

Messages delivered through CompuServe Mail include several pieces of information either specified by the sender or automatically generated by CompuServe. (Again, this is true on most commercial services.) In addition to the context of my message, for example, Figure 6.4 shows the date and time this electronic letter was transmitted: 09-Feb-91 21:55 EST (or 9:55 p.m.). CompuServe automatically attached this information to the message when it delivered it to my mailbox. Similarly, the From field, identifying the sender of this message, was automatically generated by CompuServe. The To and Subject fields, on the other hand, represent information I provided while composing this particular letter.

Deleting Unwanted Messages

After delivering my mail, CompuServe displays an Action prompt, asking what I want to do in response to this message. I could use the SEND option to compose a response to its sender. However, I really don't feel like continuing this one-person dialogue, so I'll simply delete the current message.

▶ *To delete this message:*

Type   DELETE

Press   *Enter*

After deleting the message, CompuServe redisplays its Mail prompt, as shown in Figure 6.5. Why did I do this? Simple. Because most commercial services, including CompuServe, charge a storage fee for holding on to old mail. This is fair, since the disk space required to store these messages has value. To avoid these charges, therefore, it's usually a good idea to delete any unneeded messages from your electronic in-basket.

97

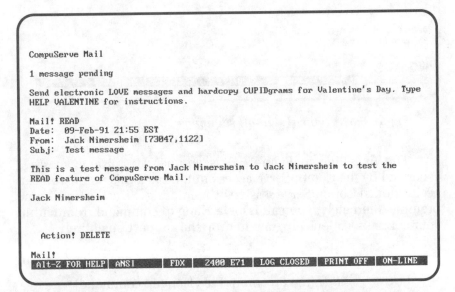

```
CompuServe Mail

1 message pending

Send electronic LOVE messages and hardcopy CUPIDgrams for Valentine's Day. Type
HELP VALENTINE for instructions.

Mail! READ
Date:  09-Feb-91 21:55 EST
From:  Jack Nimersheim [73047,1122]
Subj:  Test message

This is a test message from Jack Nimersheim to Jack Nimersheim to test the
READ feature of CompuServe Mail.

Jack Nimersheim


  Action! DELETE

Mail!
Alt-Z FOR HELP | ANSI |   FDX  | 2400 E71 | LOG CLOSED | PRINT OFF | ON-LINE
```

Figure 6.5 To avoid storage charges, it's always a good idea to delete old messages once you no longer need them.

Signing Off CompuServe

I could do much more in Mail. For now, however, let's sign off CompuServe and examine this powerful on-line activity off-line, where we won't be forced to pay access charges.

▶ *To sign off CompuServe:*

Type   BYE

Press   *Enter*

At this point, your screen should resemble Figure 6.6, which shows the sign-off sequence.

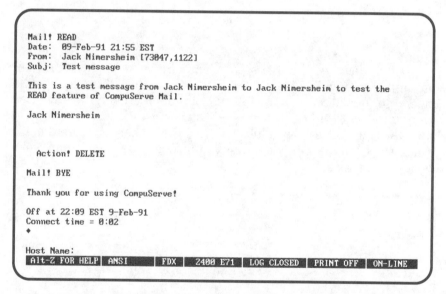

```
Mail! READ
Date:  09-Feb-91 21:55 EST
From:  Jack Nimersheim [73047,1122]
Subj:  Test message

This is a test message from Jack Nimersheim to Jack Nimersheim to test the
READ feature of CompuServe Mail.

Jack Nimersheim


  Action! DELETE

Mail! BYE

Thank you for using CompuServe!

Off at 22:09 EST 9-Feb-91
Connect time = 0:02
♦

Host Name:
Alt-Z FOR HELP  ANSI      FDX    2400 E71   LOG CLOSED   PRINT OFF   ON-LINE
```

Figure 6.6 A typical sign-off sequence.

The final line in Figure 6.6 is another Host Name message generated by the CompuServe access number. At this point, you can begin another CompuServe session by reentering CIS at the Host Name prompt. Alternately, you can issue a Hangup command from within your communications program to drop the connection entirely.

▶ *To drop the CompuServe connection with Procomm Plus, I would:*

Press   *Alt-H* (the Procomm Plus Hangup command)

As this final step demonstrates, signing off from a service is often a two-step process:

1. First, issue the appropriate command to end the current session on that service. (CompuServe accomplishes this with the Bye command.)
2. Next, unless your service automatically drops connnection at sign-off, you need to drop the connection between your modem and the access number you called. (In Procomm Plus, I accomplished this with the Alt-H Hangup command.)

The first step above stops the clock on the access charges you pay to use a commercial service like CompuServe. The second step is even more critical if, as is true in my case, you must contact that service using a long-distance access number. (Forgetting to disconnect my modem from the CompuServe access number would quickly elevate my monthly phone bills, which are already excessive enough.)

Now that we're off-line (and, therefore, off the clock), let's examine some additional aspects of electronic messaging, an awareness that increases the effectiveness and decreases the cost of your on-line communications.

E-Mail Strategies

You can use several tricks of the trade to simplify your electronic messaging. These can range from taking advantage of obscure commands and procedures supported by virtually all commercial information services to purchasing a special program designed to manage E-mail operations on a given service. In this section I'll briefly examine a few of the options you might consider when deciding on the most efficient way to organize your E-mail transactions.

Broadcast Distribution

Most E-mail services provide a simple method for sending a single message to several recipients. As a rule, this involves entering multiple user IDs at the To prompt, separated by a semicolon, space, or some other punctuation mark or nontext character. If I had wanted to transmit the message shown in Figure 6.4 to several individuals, for example, I could have structured my To field as follows:

```
To: 73047,1122; 12345,6789; 7654,321
```

Some services take this a step further by allowing you to establish broadcast groups, predefined lists of names and user IDs that are inserted at the To prompt with a single command. This feature is especially useful for anyone who regularly transmits messages to the same group of people, as would be the case, for example, when a district sales manager uses E-mail to communicate with his or her field representatives.

Coordinate On-Line Activities Off-Line

You may have noticed that, in the two exercises in which we've contacted a commercial service, I tried to get you to sign off as quickly as possible. This isn't because I dislike being on-line. In truth, I love telecommunications. Given my druthers, I'd spend a good portion of each day on-line, if this were practical. Unfortunately, it isn't.

Remember, however, that each minute you spend on-line carries some associated cost. This may include a service's normal per-minute subscribers fee, the connect charge levied by a packet-switching network (if you use one) or, as is true in my situation, the cost of a long-distance phone call to a nonlocal, local access number. Over time, as I implied at the end of the previous section, these costs mount up. One way to fend off the financial blow of telecommunicating is to organize your on-line operations off-line, when the clock isn't ticking.

This may wound your pride, but the slowest component in your PC system is you. How long does it take you to write a coherent letter? If you're like me, the answer to this question is probably several minutes. So why write that letter on-line, when you're paying someone for the time it requires to do so? Doesn't it makes more sense to gather your thoughts and compose your message *before* signing on to a commercial information or E-mail service?

Many services provide their subscribers with a personal workspace to which they can upload messages and files for additional processing. DELPHI, for example, allows you to easily transmit files stored in your personal workspace to one or more subscribers with a single SEND command. It's possible, therefore, to reduce on-line charges by using the following procedures to organize your E-mail:

1. Take all the time you want composing a letter off-line, using your favorite word processor.

2. Save that letter in ASCII (straight text) format, the most universal file format used for E-mail transactions. Depending on how your word processor works, you may need to use a file-conversion utility to convert your original letter into an ASCII file.

3. Sign on to the commercial service and immediately upload this file to your personal workspace.

4. Transfer this file from your workspace to an individual recipient or broadcast group, using the appropriate procedures for that service.

5. Sign off the service quickly, thus limiting your access charges.

Running this same scenario in reverse (i.e., quickly transferring your incoming mail from the remote system to a disk file on your own PC) will cut down the costs associated with receiving and reading messages sent to you from other users.

Using a Front-End Program

101

A variation on the previous theme is to use a front-end program designed to simplify electronic messaging on a specific service. As I mentioned earlier, the least efficient factor in any on-line session is you—or, more correctly, your human limitations. If typing a typical letter takes you several minutes, and you compose all your messages on-line, then using a commercial service or dedicated E-mail company for regular correspondence can be an expensive proposition, indeed. Using a front-end access program can minimize the cost of telecommunications by allowing you to perform the majority of your on-line activities...well...off-line.

Different front-end access programs are designed to work with different on-line information services. One such program is TAPCIS, from Software Group, Inc., which allows you to automate many activities you'd normally perform on CompuServe. Figure 6.7 shows the TAPCIS Main Menu screen. As you can see, this particular front-end program offers a wide range of options for automating the CompuServe activities you'd otherwise be forced to perform on-line.

TAPCIS includes a built-in word processor that composes messages destined for other CompuServe users. The advantage to composing your messages with TAPCIS is that you do it off-line, at your convenience, when the clock isn't ticking away connect charges. TAPCIS also lets you create a user file, containing the names and CompuServe user IDs of people who you regularly send messages to.

(TAPCIS uses this information to identify individual users, thereby ensuring that your messages get sent to the correct mailing address.) After a message is written and addressed properly, entering a single command tells TAPCIS to call your local CompuServe access number, move to Mail (or any one of the more than 50 user Forums CompuServe supports), send that message to the specified individual, and then end the current session and disconnect your phone line. Since TAPCIS performs all these activities automatically (i.e., without user intervention), your on-line—and, therefore, billable—time is kept to a minimum. Additional operations TAPCIS automates include downloading messages sent to you over CompuServe, monitoring conversations and conferences in the various CompuServe user Forums, and simplifying on-line research by quickly retrieving threads of related information appearing in multiple messages.

102

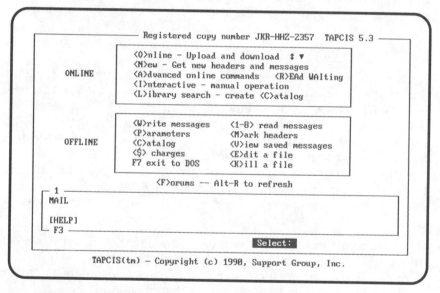

Figure 6.7 TAPCIS is one example of a front-end program that can automate CompuServe procedures.

Other front-end access programs that perform similar yeoman's duty for competing information services are available. Aladdin, for example, is designed to automate GEnie access, while Lotus Express endows MCI Mail subscribers with similar capabilities. In short, if you use a specific on-line service, it behooves you to investigate whether there's a front-end access program available for it. This is one category of software that will quickly pay for itself several times over in increased efficiency and reduced billing charges.

As these few examples illustrate, several options exist for limiting the amount of time and, by extension, money you spend on-line sending and receiving electronic mail. The potential savings associated with these options may not seem like much now. Wait until you receive that first whopping monthly bill after being bitten by the modem bug, however, and see if you don't start looking for every way possible to save a few pennies here and there. Maybe the previous suggestions can help.

Real-Time Conferencing

If sending and receiving electronic mail is cost-efficient and sensible, *real-time conferencing* can best be described as just plain fun. Admittedly, "chatting" with other people on-line can also be pragmatic, businesslike, illuminating, educational, and practical. However, the real joy associated with real-time conferencing is the simple act of meeting and getting to know new friends who drop by occasionally to visit your new electronic community.

103

On-line get-togethers can be informal—as would be the case, for instance, if you accessed your favorite service and noticed someone you wanted to chat with had signed on at the same time. On the other hand, they can also be more structured. As I've mentioned previously, for example, I and several other professional and promising wordsmiths get together in the DELPHI Writers Group every Thursday night to discuss our shared interests.

Sure, we talk about professional matters; which publishers are interested in what types of projects, what editors have recently relocated to a different magazine, how to compose and submit an effective query letter, and the like. If the truth be known, however, we also have a good time. Jokes migrate through the phone lines like Caribou crossing the Canadian wilderness. We're just as likely to discuss puns as likely as punctuation. (If you don't believe me, drop by some Thursday night at 9:30; all are welcome.)

With that informal invitation out of the way, let's examine some items relating to real-time conferencing that you should be aware of, before participating in your first on-line chat. None of these are really earth-shattering, but some idea of what to expect can help you feel more comfortable, should you decide to join in the fun.

On-Line Shorthand

I know I've said this before, but it deserves repeating: Telecommunications is a pay-as-you-play proposition. Whenever you call your favorite commercial service, it's a sure bet that someone, somewhere, is charging you something. On-line regulars have come up with a number of creative ways for limiting the costs of on-line activities, primarily by reducing either the time or the number of characters it takes us to express ourselves.

Down through the years, a veritable dictionary of special abbreviations and acronyms has sprung up around this philosophy. To anyone new to telecommunications, these various terms and phrases probably resemble a foreign language. (In fact, I know they do. Hardly a Thursday night goes by that some new participant on our weekly DELPHI conference doesn't inquire into the meaning of some cryptic verbiage employed by me or one of my fellow regulars.) And so, in the interest of initiating the uninitiated, allow me to present "A Beginner's Guide to On-Line Slang"—an informal Berlitz course, if you will, covering some of the more esoteric jargon and buzz words you're liable to encounter when participating in a real-time conference.

- ▶ *ASAP (As Soon As Possible).* This familiar acronym, which pops up regularly in electronic messages or during on-line conferences, provides the perfect example of why such slang has invaded telecommunications. It communicates an idea with four letters that otherwise would require a 20-character entry. When access charges are ticking away, such frugality can save a lot of money.

- ▶ *... (ellipsis).* Used to indicate that the sender plans to continue his or her remarks in a subsequent entry. Most services limit individual entries to approximately two lines of text, after which you must press the Enter key and transmit your comment to the conference. If you are trying to communicate a thought that exceeds this length, ending one comment with an ellipsis tells people that additional text relating to the current entry will follow.

- ▶ *BRB (Be Right Back).* Used whenever someone temporarily departs an on-line conference. When other participants in the conference see this abbreviation, they know not to address comments to or expect responses from that individual until he or she returns.

▶ *BTW (By The Way)*. Used just as it would be in normal conversation. For example:

```
BTW, I chatted with Bob yesterday and he's feeling
better.
```

▶ *FYI (For Your Information)*. Yes, this inane abbreviation has crossed over from Corporate America to telecommunications.

▶ *GA (Go Ahead)*. A form of on-line etiquette. Commonly used at the end of a multiline entry (see the ellipsis code, above) to inform the other participants that the writer has finished his or her entire thought. Another common use for the GA code is when several people are attempting to type at the same time, which usually results in confusion. In this situation, one or more individuals may elect to hold their own thoughts in abeyance and defer to a fellow participant by typing GA.

▶ *<grin> (or, alternately, <g>)*. Used to end a comment offered in jest. Since people chatting on-line are unable to enjoy the luxury of analyzing visual or verbal signals (clues humans rely on to ascertain the true meaning behind someone's words when conversing face-to-face), using this code will help ensure that others do not misinterpret your remarks. In sum, to avoid offending someone with a humorous remark, end it with the <grin> code, as in:

```
Jane, is that garbage you're transmitting line noise,
or are you studying a foreign language in night school?
<grin>
```

   BTW: Always enclose a grin code in greater than/less than symbols (<>), as shown in the previous example, so people realize it is code, rather than part of your actual comment.

▶ *IMHO or IMO (In My Humble Opinion)*. This comment is used as it would be in normal conversation, with one caveat. As Michael Banks, a good friend and fellow writer, once pointed out to me, people who rely on this phrase too much while participating in on-line conferences tend to deliver their messages while precariously perched atop some type of soapbox. Beware the IMHO people; it's not uncommon for them to confuse their humble opinions with arrogance.

105

▶ *LOL (Lots Of Laughter or Laughing Out Loud)*. If someone says something funny or entertaining during an on-line conversation, you may want to let them know you appreciate their wit. A simple LOL should suffice.

▶ *OTF (On The Floor)*. The highest on-line compliment you can offer someone in response to a humorous remark. Use this shorthand notation instead of LOL, should someone enter something that really tickles your funny bone.

In addition to these basic slang terms, telecommunications veterans also rely on special ASCII characters to clarify or, in some cases, simply embellish the appearance of their on-line repartee. One of the most common applications of this technique is to direct a comment to one of several people participating in an on-line conference. To accomplish this, precede your comment with a greater than symbol (>) and that person's name, as illustrated in the following example:

```
> MIKE, I couldn't agree more.
```

A variation of this theme is to add several dashes before the greater than symbol. This technique is especially useful if the service you are accessing uses greater than symbols to identify individual speakers, as explained in the next paragraph. Adding dashes under these circumstances guarantees that the person to whom you are directing a comment recognizes your intentions, as in the following example:

```
NIMS>  ---> MIKE, I couldn't agree more.
```

As I mentioned in the previous paragraph, some services distinguish among the different participants in a real-time conference by automatically preceding each on-line comment with the name of the person who entered it. Flip-flopping the previous notation, therefore, provides a simple way to identify a remark made about yourself. One example of how this technique is used is:

```
NIMS> <---feeling real tired right now.
```

A few paragraphs earlier, I pointed out how conference participants often use a <grin> message to identify a comment made in jest. A more picturesque variation of this same theme is to end your comical comment with a colon, followed by a right parenthesis, as in:

```
I notice Bill didn't sign on tonight. His phone bill
must have arrived today. :)
```

What does this cryptic symbol mean? Cock your head to the left and take another look at it, sideways. Now do you understand?

There you have it, "A Beginner's Guide to On-Line Slang." While there is no rule that states you must use these various terms and techniques in your own on-line activities, a basic familiarity will help avoid any confusion you might experience during a real-time conference, should one or more of them pop up—as they undoubtedly will. If this happens, at least you'll know what's going on.

Courtesy Counts

For all of its positive attributes, telecommunicating has one major shortcoming: It can be extremely one-dimensional. When we traditionally converse, we tend to rely on more than words to communicate. For example, whether by design or instinct, most of us interpret body language, which in turn helps us analyze the true meaning behind spoken words. Vocal inflection also provides valuable clues to someone's intent when we engage in face-to-face conversation.

These subtle overtones do not manifest themselves into electronic conversation. Consequently, you must be extra careful that the purpose of your prose is fully understood. That's one valuable function of the various shorthand expressions introduced in the previous section.

A second potential peril associated with the impersonal quality of real-time conferencing is a tendency to forget that the people on the other end of a connection are also real, live individuals, individuals with feelings and, in some cases, problems or fragile egos of their own. I've watched people I know well take on an entirely new and not very endearing persona in the impersonal environment of a real-time conference.

These observations are not meant to inhibit you. As is true of any interactive forum, you should feel free to express yourself completely in a real-time conference. A little empathy and diplomacy can go a long way, however, toward making that conference an enjoyable experience for everyone involved. I found it helpful to look at being welcomed into an on-line conversation as the electronic analogy of being invited to a party. If you're considerate of and courteous to your fellow guests, they'll extend the same consideration and courtesy to you.

107

However, the best way to learn about real-time conferences is to participate in one. You are encouraged to stop by our Writer's Group conference some Thursday night. By way of a formal invitation, let me to outline the specific steps it takes to get there. First, use your communications software to sign on to DELPHI and get to the Opening menu. (See Appendix A for information on how to contact DELPHI to subscribe.)

 To access the Writer's Conference:

Type	GROUP WRITERS
Press	*Enter*
Type	CONFERENCE
Press	*Enter*
Type	WHO
Press	*Enter*

The previous step displays a listing of those individuals participating in our weekly get-together on a particular Thursday night, as well as the conference number DELPHI has assigned to that evening's festivities.

 To join us:

Type	*the conference number displayed in response to your WHO command*
Press	*Enter*

We'll be notified that you've entered our little group, and you'll probably see several personal welcome messages from the various people signed on that night. Then, simply sit back and join in. Type in any comments, questions, observations, etc., you have that relate to the topic of the night. When you press Enter, your words will magically appear on our screens. If you have questions about any DELPHI commands or procedures, feel free to ask them also. Someone will graciously provide assistance. First, relax and have fun. That, after all, is what real-time conferencing is all about.

What You've Learned

▶ Electronic messaging resembles the more familiar postal service, both in what it does and how it works. Sending messages electronically, however, can be more efficient and less expensive than traditional mail. Especially useful are the front-end programs several companies sell to completely automate the process of sending electronic mail over specific on-line services.

▶ Real-time conferencing is one of the more interesting and enjoyable on-line activities you can participate in, once you have a modem connected to your PC.

109

File Transfers

In This Chapter

▶ *What is a file transfer*

▶ *Shareware and public-domain software*

▶ *File-transfer protocols*

▶ *Initiating a file transfer*

▶ *Guarding against computer viruses*

Perhaps the most practical application of modem communications is the exchange of files between two computers. In this chapter, I'll begin by explaining how file transfers work. Next, I'll discuss some of the different types of files to which a modem gives you access. Finally, I'll outline the steps involved in a typical file transfer so you'll have an idea of what to expect when the time comes to begin transferring files with your PC.

What Is a File Transfer?

Stated simply, a file transfer is the process of copying a file from one computer to another computer, using your communications software and modem. The two systems involved in a file exchange will range in size and power; from the large mainframes found in many corporations to a laptop PC, most computers in between, or virtually any combination thereof.

Regardless of the two participating computers, the basic procedures used to transfer a file are the same. The sending computer reads the file, usually from a disk, tape, or some other storage device. As the file is read, its contents are sent to a modem, which converts this data into a series of analog signals for transmission across standard phone lines. As the modem on the other end of the phone connection receives these analog signals, it converts them back into digital form and transfers this data to the second computer, which, in turn, takes the data it receives and stores it in a file—a file that is, in essence, a mirror copy of the one which originally existed (and indeed, still exists) on the sending computer.

As you can see, file transfers are similar to FAX transmissions, another popular form of information exchange. Whereas the latter sends a printed page across a telephone line, however, the former transfers electronic data to and from your PC.

A wealth of information can be exchanged during a file transfer; from a personal data file that you share with someone in a distant city, to any of the thousands of public-domain programs and shareware packages that are available on-line. Public-domain software and shareware represent a potential source of many convenient and useful programs. As such, they are a major contributor to the current popularity of both commercial on-line services and countless BBSs that have sprung up around the country over the past few years. Given this fact, they warrant at least a brief discussion.

Has Your Modem Got a Deal for You

Computer consultants regularly advise their clients that it's realistic to spend as much on the programs they buy as they did on the hardware that runs them. Underlying this professional maxim is an undeniable truth: PC software ain't cheap. Word processors, electronic spread-sheets, database programs: the best-selling titles in every one of these software categories cost around $500 each. Prices for programs in other, more specialized areas, such as desktop publishing, computer-assisted design (CAD), and high-end graphics, can run considerably higher. At such exorbitant prices, it doesn't take long to ring up a sizable tab, when the time comes to begin purchasing the software you'll use on your PC. One practical alternative is to seek public-domain and shareware packages, many of which offer comparable capabilities at a fraction of the cost.

The difference between public domain software and shareware is more a legal matter than an indication of the quality or cost of the product. Authors of public domain software have elected to place their product in the public domain, without retaining the copyright to that work. This allows others to modify the code of that product, if they so desire.

Shareware, on the other hand, may or may not be distributed free of charge. The author, however, still retains his or her copyright—and, therefore, legal ownership—of the work. You can use and freely distribute a shareware program, but you can't change it.

113

Some shareware products are sold commercially. Others are distributed without cost. The category in which a specific package falls is generally pointed out in a sentence or two within its documentation, or on its initial display that either requests or requires payment, should you decide to use that program. If payment solicitation is requested—for example, `If you like this program, feel free to send $25...`—you are not required to pay for the program. If this stipulation is presented as a requirement—`Anyone using this program should send $25...`—then you're looking at a shareware product you must pay a licensing fee for, if you plan to use it regularly.

Manufacturers of both public-domain software and shareware encourage users to make copies of any programs they like and *share* them with their friends. (Hence, the name, *shareware*.) This differs from commercial software packages, the copying and distribution of which is blatantly illegal.

Public-domain and shareware programs believe that payment for software should be voluntary and, even then, minimal. As a rule, the people responsible for public-domain and shareware programs keep prices down by bypassing the extensive (and, therefore, expensive) manufacturing, marketing, and distribution channels that inevitably spring up around commercial software ventures. Consequently, the majority of programs in these two categories cost anywhere from nothing to around $50, a far cry from the three-figure price tag attached to most commercial software. True, their documentation may not be a glossy, four-color manual. (More commonly, it's a special DOC file included with the program that you must print out on your own printer.) And technical support—though eminently qualified, since it's usually the author himself or a member of his programming team who provides it—won't match that offered by a major manufacturer. Still, public-domain and shareware programs have come a long way since Jim Button and the late Andrew Fluegelman introduced the shareware phenomenon with their almost simultaneous release of PC-File and PC-Talk, respectively, in the early 1980s. For example, Procomm Plus, the communications program I used in several examples in this book, began as shareware. In fact, the older shareware version, simply called Procomm, is still stored on several hundred BBSs and readily available with a simple file transfer.

114

Let's begin by examining what this activity called transferring files entails. We'll start by looking at an aspect of modem communications you haven't encountered yet: file-transfer protocols.

File-Transfer Protocols

Whenever your PC exchanges a file with another computer, it must rely on some type of *file-transfer protocol* to accomplish this. Stated simply, protocols establish the digital ground rules that define the precise procedures your PC and the remote system use to coordinate the movement of data across a phone line. As an added attraction, many file-transfer protocols also include *error-checking routines*, special procedures designed to ensure that the data arriving at one computer matches the transmission from the other end of the connection.

A Myriad of Choices

Literally dozens of file-transfer protocols have evolved through the years. Rattling off all their names could send a bureaucrat into acronym shock, but the most popular include:

▶ XMODEM

▶ YMODEM

▶ ZMODEM

▶ KERMIT

▶ ASCII

▶ COMPUSERVE B+

The list goes on, and on, and on. What differentiates one from the other? There isn't a firm answer. Which is most efficient for a given situation? An explanation of how protocols differ from one another will, hopefully, help you formulate your own answer.

To understand what file-transfer protocols are and how they work, consider for a moment the rules of grammar. Whenever you see a space in this book, it's a pretty good assumption that I'm indicating the end of a word. Consider how difficult deciphering my timeless text would be if everythinglookedlikethis. Similarly, periods separate sentences while blank lines divide paragraphs, identifying discrete and, hopefully, logical segments of the overall discussion.

115

Protocols attempt to apply a similar structural paradigm to data exchange. For example, XMODEM, the granddaddy of all PC protocols, developed by Ward Christiansen, begins by breaking a file down into individual blocks, each of which is 128 characters long. (Compare this to a sentence in standard text.) It then starts transmitting that file, one block at a time, surrounding each block with additional characters designed to identify its beginning, end, block number relative to the total file, and a special checksum character that detects potential transmission errors.

Each time XMODEM sends a data block, the transmitting PC pauses to wait for a response from the computer on the other end of the line. That response can signal either success, triggering transmission of the next block, or failure, in which case the same block will be reset. (Without getting too technical, this success or failure is determined by the receiving computer comparing the results of specific calculations performed on a data block with the checksum character that accompanied it.)

Of course, in order to perform all of these steps properly, both systems involved must be using the same protocol—the same grammatical rules—within the context of a given file transfer. If the receiving system is set up to use the YMODEM protocol, for example, which relies on 1K data blocks rather than the 128-byte block structure supported by XMODEM, you can understand how major problems might arise. This would be comparable to suddenly deciding to use capital X's to separate individual words in this book, causing myXtextXtoXlookXlikeXthis. Not a very efficient method of communication, is it?

Retiring the Old Guard

Although it's still the most prevalent file-transfer protocol supported by PC communications programs, XMODEM is beginning to show its age. While more and more PCs access mainframe computers, XMODEM's usefulness continues to diminish. Many mainframe computers are limited to 7-bit operations, in which 7 bits of data represent individual characters. Consequently, they can't communicate using XMODEM's 8-bit data structure. Additionally, transferring files with XMODEM can be a slow process—an unavoidable result of its reliance on small data blocks and all the back-and-forth communications XMODEM depends on for error correction.

In the old days, when 300- or even 1200-baud modems dominated the communications market, protocol efficiency exerted only a minimal influence on the total time required to transfer a file. Today, with modems supporting communications at 2400 or 9600 bps (and even higher) gaining in popularity, XMODEM's speed—or, more correctly, lack thereof—has become a ponderous liability.

YMODEM was one of the earliest alternatives to evolve from the original XMODEM protocol. (X becomes Y, get it?) YMODEM increases the size of each data block transmitted from 128 bytes to 1K. This modification alone dramatically improves performance, due primarily to YMODEM's capability to transfer a 1K data block (i.e., peel off data, transmit it, verify error-free reception, and then move on) in a single step, compared to the eight steps XMODEM needs to transfer an equal amount of data.

In addition to dramatically decreasing the time required for file transfers, YMODEM brings a touch of convenience to the process. Unlike XMODEM, which is limited to transferring files one at a time, YMODEM sends multiple files in a single pass. As each file transfers, YMODEM automatically passes its name, along with a date and time stamp, to the receiving system.

116

However, YMODEM's improvements can be a double-edged sword. Should errors arise during a data-block transfer, it takes YMODEM eight times longer to retransmit the troublesome 1K of data than it would a 128-byte XMODEM block. For this reason, YMODEM protocol proves an inefficient alternative, if your local phone system (or any phone link between it and the computer you're calling, for that matter) is plagued by excessive line noise—as many of today's phone systems still are.

The next major advance in PC-to-PC file transfers was the introduction of Chuck Fosberg's ZMODEM, which uses an error-correcting, streaming protocol to improve the overall efficiency and reliability of file transfers. ZMODEM transmits files in a continuous stream, intermittently inserting error-checking codes within each file. These codes allow the receiving system to constantly evaluate data integrity. The transmitting PC waits until the entire file is sent to verify its receipt from the other system. Based on that response, questionable data is retransmitted, as necessary.

ZMODEM's biggest drawback is that it sacrifices data buffering for data streaming. Consequently, it requires a much higher level of disk access—and, therefore, more time dedicated to the relatively slow activity of reading information from a disk—to transmit a file using the ZMODEM protocol. As a rule, however, ZMODEM tends to be faster than either of its alphabetical ancestors on a file-by-file basis, especially for file transfers occurring over a noisy connection.

117

The Frog Factor

One file-transfer protocol that deserves special mention is KERMIT, developed at Columbia University in the early 1980s. Aside from the fact that KERMIT was actually named after the popular Muppet character, Kermit the Frog, it fully supports file transfers between PCs and mainframe computers that rely exclusively on a 7-bit data structure. You should know, however, that KERMIT tends to be a painfully slow protocol. If another option is available, therefore, consider using it. In some circumstances, however, KERMIT may be the only standard protocol that will work.

I say *standard* because many companies that use mainframe computers rely on self-written protocols to manage file transfers between their systems and a PC in the field. Anyone with the appropriate knowledge and enough effort can design a protocol that will work with a specific combination of systems, in a given situation. Perhaps the prime example of this is COMPUSERVE B+, a proprietary protocol developed by CompuServe to manage file transfers over that popular commercial information service. Given CompuServe's subscriber base of approximately 650,000, it's no surprise that several major communications programs, including Procomm Plus, have incorporated COMPUSERVE B+ into the list of protocols they support. COMPUSERVE B+ is an extremely fast protocol. For transferring files to and from CompuServe, therefore, it is a natural choice, if your communications program supports it.

Difficult Choices

As you can see, the subject of file-transfer protocols is a complex one. Alternatives and options abound. So, which is the most appropriate protocol for a given situation? At the risk of sounding like I'm copping out, it depends on the situation.

If the computer you want to call supports only a single protocol, then you really have no choice. Since it is necessary to have both machines use the same protocol for any file transfer to be successful, your only option is to match the one available on the remote system. A similar situation exists when you're exchanging files with a mainframe that can't support an 8-bit data structure and does not provide a propriety protocol, in which case KERMIT is the most likely candidate. When alternatives are available, however, the decision becomes more difficult, and depends on several contributing factors.

The quality of the connection certainly comes into play, given the negative impact line noise can have on, for example, YMODEM transfers. The number of files you're transferring will also influence your decision. Using a single-file protocol like XMODEM to transmit a long list of files, one at a time, simply doesn't make sense if a multifile protocol like YMODEM or KERMIT is available as an alternative. In the end, understanding how different protocols work, and recognizing the advantages and disadvantages associated with each, is the best way to guarantee you'll choose the most efficient protocol for a specific purpose.

Enough of this technical stuff. You've probably been champing at the bit (pardon my pun) to go back on-line and try your first file transfer. Okay, let's do it.

A Typical File Transfer

File transfer is a two-way street. That is, you can either send a file transfer on your PC to a remote system or have the remote system send a file to you. Each of these procedures is called by a different name.

▶ *Uploading* files consists of transmitting data from your PC to the remote system.

▶ *Downloading* files involves moving data in the opposite direction (i.e., from the remote system to your PC).

The same basic steps are used to exchange data between your PC and another computer, regardless of whether you're uploading or downloading a file. In either case, you would:

1. Call and sign on to the remote system, using your communications software.

2. Identify the file you want to download or, alternately, the location on the remote system you want to upload a file to.

3. Select a suitable protocol for this transfer and configure both computers accordingly.

4. Tell the remote system to begin uploading or downloading the file, as appropriate.

5. Use your communications program to complete the transfer on your end of the connection.

The exact procedures used to initiate the last three steps vary from system to system and within different PC communications programs. To give you a general idea of how file-transfers work, however, let's look at a typical Procomm Plus session that includes downloading a file from CompuServe, using the XMODEM protocol. We'll pick up this sample session after you successfully sign on to CompuServe and get to the top-level menu.

119

> ▶ **Note:** Once again, I'm using CompuServe in this exercise because of that system's status as the commercial on-line service with the most subscribers. Also, as pointed out in the previous chapter, many modems and communications programs include a trial subscription to CompuServe. If you do not belong to CompuServe, or use a program other than Procomm Plus, don't panic. The following exercise will still demonstrate the general procedures used to exchange files between your PC and a remote system.

The file we want to download is located in the on-line technical support area for Datastorm, the company that manufactures Procomm Plus. As outlined in the previous chapter, CompuServe resembles other commercial information services in that accessing a specific user area is a simple matter of selecting the appropriate sequence of options from its multilevel menu structure.

> ▶ **Note:** From time to time, CompuServe adds new services or deletes old ones, in an attempt to keep up with its subscribers' interests. It's possible, therefore, that the option number associated with a particular user area or forum will have changed since I've finished this book. For this reason, I have included a brief description of the option number you should select. Always check that description, to verify that you are selecting the correct option.

120

The Datastorm area is in the PC Software Forum, which is listed under the Computers/Technology user area.

 To enter the PC Software Forum:

Type   11
Press   *Enter*

This selects the Computers/Technology option. Then,

Type   1
Press   *Enter*

This selects the Software Forum option. Notice that the Datastorm Forum is identified as one of the options on this menu. This is where you'll find the file I plan to download. To access this user area:

Type   *the number corresponding to the Datastorm Forum*
Press   *Enter*

At this point, you must tell CompuServe that you want to join the Datastorm Forum. We'll use a shortcut command to accomplish this.

To join the Datastorm Forum:

Type   JOIN
Press   *Enter*

You are then asked to provide some information about yourself. Go ahead and do this. It costs nothing to join a CompuServe forum, and members of different forums have access to a wide range of information on various PC hardware and software products.

After you've entered all the requested information, the screen advances to the Datastorm Forum menu. From here you can select LIBRARIES, the area within individual forums in which CompuServe stores most of its downloadable files.

 To select the LIBRARIES option:

Type   3
Press   *Enter*

 To reach the file we want to download, which is located in the General Help library:

Type   1
Press   *Enter*

At this point, several options are available. Because we ultimately want to download a file, let's begin by viewing a directory of the files in the General Help area.

▶ *To view the Datastorm File directory:*

Type   2
Press   *Enter*

After a few seconds, a file listing should begin appearing on your Display screen, similar to the one shown in Figure 7.1.

There should be a file on your screen called PC-CIS.TXT, a short (7K) text file that explains how to configure your CompuServe user profile for 8-bit operations.

We'll use the XMODEM protocol to transfer this PC-CIS.TXT file to your PC. First, however, go back to the Datastorm options menu.

```
BBSINT.HLP/binary        08-Feb-90 13312          Accesses: 118
VERSIO.TXT/binary        08-Feb-90 3547           Accesses: 282
NOISE.TXT/binary         07-Feb-90 8064           Accesses: 175
NONOIS.ARC/binary        07-Feb-90 4096           Accesses: 215
PRCMJR.ARC/binary        07-Feb-90 3945           Accesses: 13
SERCBL.ARC/binary        07-Feb-90 4372           Accesses: 104
PCNEWS.N01               03-Jan-90 17443          Accesses: 321
PC-CIS.ARC/binary        11-Oct-89 3708           Accesses: 578
PC-CIS.TXT               11-Oct-89 7458           Accesses: 261

[73707,1100]
HELPCP.ARC/binary        07-Jul-89 9480           Accesses: 370
QANDA.TXT                23-Mar-89 25266          Accesses: 931
UPLDHE.TXT               02-Mar-89 8064           Accesses: 258
COMHEL.ARC/binary        24-Feb-89 80641          Accesses: 146
WHTSNW.TXT               18-Jan-89 5663           Accesses: 626

[74216,1077]
PSW.ARC/binary           03-Jan-89 53162          Accesses: 764

[73707,1100]
ZHOWTO.ARC/binary        22-Dec-88 4096           Accesses: 1365

Press <CR> !
```
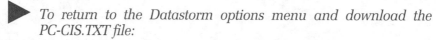
`Alt-Z FOR HELP | ANSI | FDX | 2400 E71 | LOG CLOSED | PRINT OFF | ON-LINE`

122

Figure 7.1 A sample file listing from CompuServe's Datastorm area.

▶ *To return to the Datastorm options menu and download the PC-CIS.TXT file:*

Press *Enter at the end of each Listing screen until you return to the Datastorm options menu.*

Then,

Type 4

Press *Enter to select the DOWNLOAD option*

At this point, CompuServe asks for the name of the file you want to download.

Type `PC-CIS.TXT`

Press *Enter*

You are then given a list of file-transfer protocols from which to choose, as shown in Figure 7.2. As mentioned earlier, we'll use XMODEM.

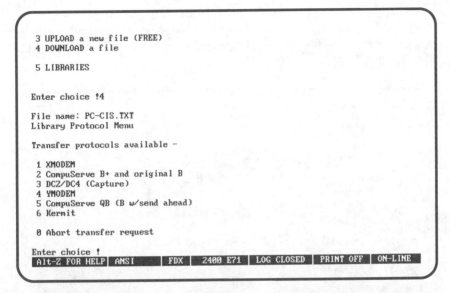

```
 3 UPLOAD a new file (FREE)
 4 DOWNLOAD a file

 5 LIBRARIES


Enter choice !4

File name: PC-CIS.TXT
Library Protocol Menu

Transfer protocols available -

 1 XMODEM
 2 CompuServe B+ and original B
 3 DC2/DC4 (Capture)
 4 YMODEM
 5 CompuServe QB (B w/send ahead)
 6 Kermit

 0 Abort transfer request

Enter choice !
```
| Alt-Z FOR HELP | ANSI | FDX | 2400 E71 | LOG CLOSED | PRINT OFF | ON-LINE |

Figure 7.2 *Most information services support multiple file-transfer protocols.*

123

▶ *To specify an XMODEM file transfer:*

Type   1
Press   *Enter*

CompuServe informs you that it is starting an XMODEM Send, and instructs you to initiate a similar receive on your end.

▶ *To initiate a download with Procomm Plus:*

Press   *PgDn*

This displays the Procomm Plus File-Transfer Protocol Selection screen, as shown in Figure 7-3. You use this screen to identify which protocol you wish to use for the current file transfer.

▶ *To specify XMODEM:*

Type   X
Press   *Enter*

This displays the Procomm Plus Receive XMODEM input box, shown in Figure 7.4. You use this screen to specify the name you want the downloaded file to be, when it transfers to your system. We'll call this test file TEST.TXT.

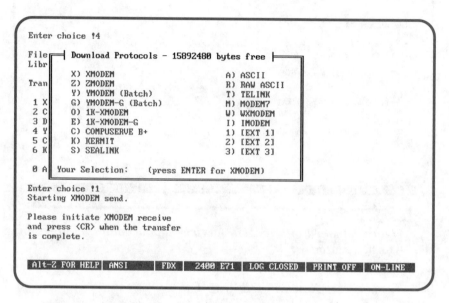

```
Enter choice !4

File┌─┤ Download Protocols - 15892480 bytes free ├──┐
Libr│                                                │
     │   X) XMODEM                A) ASCII            │
Tran │   Z) ZMODEM                R) RAW ASCII        │
     │   Y) YMODEM (Batch)        T) TELINK           │
 1 X │   G) YMODEM-G (Batch)      M) MODEM7           │
 2 C │   O) 1K-XMODEM             W) WXMODEM          │
 3 D │   E) 1K-XMODEM-G           I) IMODEM           │
 4 Y │   C) COMPUSERVE B+         1) [EXT 1]          │
 5 C │   K) KERMIT                2) [EXT 2]          │
 6 K │   S) SEALINK               3) [EXT 3]          │
     │                                                │
 0 A │ Your Selection:    (press ENTER for XMODEM)    │
     └────────────────────────────────────────────────┘

Enter choice !1
Starting XMODEM send.

Please initiate XMODEM receive
and press <CR> when the transfer
is complete.

│ Alt-Z FOR HELP │ ANSI │  FDX │ 2400 E71 │ LOG CLOSED │ PRINT OFF │ ON-LINE │
```

Figure 7.3 Pressing PgDn displays the Procomm Plus Protocol Selection screen.

 *To name the file:*

Type   TEST.TXT

Press   *Enter*

At this point, a special window appears on your display. It should contain information about the current download operation, including such items as protocol selected, file name, byte count, block count, error count, and progress, among others. Exactly which of these fields will contain information depends on whether you are uploading or downloading a file. Some of these fields, specifically the byte count and block count values, will be updated constantly during a file transfer, thus allowing you to keep track of the progress of the current transfer.

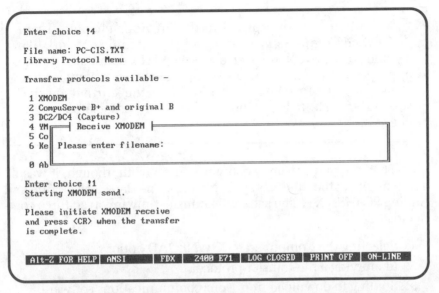

```
Enter choice !4

File name: PC-CIS.TXT
Library Protocol Menu

Transfer protocols available -

1 XMODEM
2 CompuServe B+ and original B
3 DC2/DC4 (Capture)
4 YM┌──┤ Receive XMODEM ├──────────────────────────┐
5 Co│                                               │
6 Ke│  Please enter filename:                       │
   │                                               │
0 Ab└───────────────────────────────────────────────┘

Enter choice !1
Starting XMODEM send.

Please initiate XMODEM receive
and press <CR> when the transfer
is complete.


│Alt-Z FOR HELP│ ANSI    │    FDX │  2400 E71 │ LOG CLOSED │ PRINT OFF │ ON-LINE │
```

125

Figure 7.4 Like most communications programs, Procomm Plus lets you assign a name to the file you're downloading.

When the requested file is transferred, your system will sound a beep. After a few seconds, the transfer window disappears and you return to the CompuServe screen. At this point, press Enter to tell CompuServe that the file transfer is finished.

 To terminate this file transfer:

Press   *Enter*

This returns you to the DataStorm options menu. From here, you could perform additional operations in the Datastorm Forum or, if you wanted to, access other CompuServe areas. Instead, since we've accomplished our goal, let's sign off CompuServe.

 To sign off CompuServe:

Type   BYE

Press   *Enter*

> ⊘ **Caution:** As you learned in the previous chapter, if you called CompuServe over a packet-switching network like Tymnet or SprintNet, enter a +++ ATH0 command or the appropriate Hangup command supported by your communications software to completely terminate the current on-line session and shut down the clock on any associated access charges.

That may have seemed complicated. In truth, though, it wasn't. The majority of the time was spent getting to the Datastorm Forum and finding PC-CIS.TXT. The actual file transfer only involved three commands:

1. Selecting the CompuServe DOWNLOAD option.
2. Identifying a file-transfer protocol.
3. Starting to download from your communications software.

Your reward for these efforts? A copy of PC-CIS.TXT transferred from CompuServe's mainframe computer in Columbus, Ohio, to your PC. And you could just as easily have copied a shareware database program, or a game in the public domain, or any one of several thousand other files available from the different CompuServe user forums. Furthermore, with only minor variations, these same procedures download files stored on virtually any commercial on-line service or local BBS. But before you start madly copying every file you find on every remote system you contact, I would be remiss if I didn't inform you about a skeleton in the on-line closet of which you should be aware.

Computer Viruses

There is no diplomatic way to put this, so I'll just come right out and say it: There are ruthless modem owners out there who get their jollies by messing up someone else's PC. They do so by creating and disseminating destructive bits of code, called *computer viruses*. As a rule, these reprehensible idiots attempt to spread their wares using the very same channels legitimate programmers rely on to distribute public-domain and shareware products (i.e., commercial information services and locally organized electronic bulletin boards).

The general phrase *computer virus* is popularly (and mistakenly) used to describe several varieties of potentially destructive code. These include bombs, true viruses, and worms, to name but three. Although they differ in how they work and what they do, each shares a common goal: They're designed solely to disrupt your PC activities. A relatively harmless virus may simply interrupt a program you're using to play a short tune and then restore the status quo, exactly as it was before it surfaced. A truly malicious virus, on the other hand, can contaminate a hard disk in a nanosecond or two. Mischievous or malevolent, computer viruses represent the darker side of telecommunications.

Bombs Away

One of the easiest pieces of destructive code to create is a *software bomb*. This type of virus can sneak into your system disguised as a relatively innocuous program—one that plays a short tune, or displays a cute picture, or some other, equally frivolous activity. As you're diverted by the bomb's subterfuge, however, it may be preparing to wipe out your hard disk's directory or file allocation table. Those who disseminate software bombs seem to enjoy bragging about their brainless acts. It's not unusual for one of these programs to display some sort of contemptuous message—Hah! Gotcha! or some similar piece of inanity—before the bomb explodes and does its dirty deed.

Slightly more elegant, and infinitely more nefarious, is the *logic bomb*. Unlike software bombs, which start off fluffy and go off with a bang (thus living up to their sobriquet), logic bombs infiltrate your system disguised as a useful program. The bomb then sits idle until activated by an external event—a predetermined date, the selection of an obscure menu option, or some such catalyst. Once triggered, a logic bomb wreaks havoc quickly and maliciously. Particularly vile are the designers of these programs who try to pass themselves off as legitimate shareware distributors, promising productivity and then delivering destruction.

Vindictive Viruses

True viruses up the ante from software and logic bombs. Mimicking their namesake, computer viruses enter your system and then begin reproducing, often attaching themselves to popular commercial application programs. Once it has embedded itself within a program, a virus

127

is virtually undetectable. This makes a virus extremely difficult to identify and even harder to eliminate. Worse still, a single virus entering your system can replicate itself several times, within several different programs, shortly after invading your PC. Expunging a virus from one application, therefore, does not guarantee that you've eradicated it your entire system. One of its clones may still lurk within a different program.

Another consequence of a viral infection is that, even if the virus itself is not destructive, its very presence adversely influences system performance. For example, each time a virus replicates itself, it actually increases the size of whatever program file it infects. Over time, all this superfluous code can slow down disk access and, in some cases, the speed with which the application itself executes.

The Wicked Worm

Worms and viruses are close cousins. Biologically speaking, if you will, a worm is nothing more than a neutered virus. A worm looks and performs almost exactly like a virus, except that it does not reproduce. Consequently, once a worm is detected, it's relatively easy to get rid of; one quick, clean kill and it's gone.

The worm's so-called popularity diminished greatly since the emergence of true viruses. In some perverse way, this sounds perfectly logical. Given the demented nature of anyone who would consider infecting someone else's system with destructive code a worthwhile activity, they must wonder what the sense is in creating something relatively easy to find and eliminate when a more pernicious alternative exists? Among the hot-dog hackers possessing such destructive tendencies, the true virus is truly top dog.

All Is Not Lost

Now that I've rained on your telecommunications parade, let me paint a silver lining around this particular cloud. The people responsible for managing commercial information services and local BBSs take the threat of computer viruses seriously. Most go to great lengths to avoid having potentially destructive code infiltrate their on-line offerings. Should a virus manage to evade detection and actually make its way into a commercial service or BBS system, you can bet it won't be there very long. Someone, somewhere, will report its presence, and the proper steps will be taken to keep it from spreading further. Also, you can rest assured that information on a new virus will spread quickly among the small community of legitimate BBS system operators. These individuals have dedicated themselves to sharing the joys of communicating on-line. And they'll do everything possible to protect the people that call their systems.

If cautionary steps initiated by others don't put your mind at ease, you may want to take matters into your own hands and invest in an anti-viral program. These programs, sometimes called *vaccines*, are classified into two categories: *detection software* and *prevention programs*. Stated simply, detection software identifies viruses that have already invaded your system and takes the appropriate steps to eliminate them. A prevention program, on the other hand, acts like an electronic sentry, guarding your system against initial infection.

Peter Norton, long recognized as an expert when it comes to the inner workings of IBM-compatible computers, recently released the Norton Anti-Virus. This $129.95 package contains both a detection and a prevention module. The first, a 24K terminate-and-stay-resident (TSR) program, intercepts potential viruses entering your system to alert you to their presence before your PC or disk is affected. The second module, an executable program called Viral Clinic, scans the files on your disks to identify any viruses it recognizes. If a virus is detected, you can instruct Viral Clinic to either remove the questionable file or, if possible, remove the destructive code and repair it. Anti-Virus can recognize and eliminate several well known viruses, including the infamous Jerusalem B code that recently immigrated to this country from the MidEast. Norton's Anti-Virus is but one of many impressive anti-viral utility programs currently marketed by major software companies.

Assistance in virus detection and elimination also exists outside the commercial realm. Particularly noteworthy are the efforts of The Computer Virus Industry Association, an organization based in Santa Clara, California. As one of its services, this group sponsors a national BBS that specializes in distributing information about known viruses. To contact the association's BBS, which operates 24 hours a day, configure your communications software to 300/1200/ or 2400 bps and an N,8,1 parameter setting and dial (408) 988-4004. While on-line, you can also download several shareware programs designed to protect your system against virus attack. (It's no coincidence that conscientious shareware programmers, who have seen their market turn into a popular distribution channel for viruses, dedicate a lot of time and energy to nullifying the threat of digital saboteurs. Thoughtless individuals are messing with their turf, and they don't like it.) The Computer Virus Industry Association also supports a voice line, which is available to anyone who suspects their system may have suffered a major virus infection. You can reach them at (408)727-4559 during business hours (Pacific Time).

It's impossible for me to guarantee that you'll never encounter a virus; anyone who uses a modem to exchange files with another computer runs at least a slight risk of a virus infecting their PC. (Keep in mind that downloading a file is a prerequisite for catching a virus from a remote system. Simply signing on to a system and, for example, transmitting an electronic message or participating in a real-time conference will not invite a viruse into your PC.) With a little caution, however, that risk can be minimized almost to the point of insignificance. My advice, therefore, is this: Don't let the fear of computer viruses ruin the joys associated with telecommunicating. I've been going on-line for almost a decade now, and have yet to run into any problems.

130

What You Have Learned

▶ One of the more productive uses for your modem is to transfer files to and from other computers. File transfers allow you to exchange information, both program and data files, over a convenient and inexpensive telephone connection.

▶ Public-domain programs and shareware provide an inexpensive alternative to costly commercial software. Commercial information services and local BBSs provide a clearinghouse for such programs.

▶ File-transfer protocols establish the digital ground rules that define the procedures your PC and the remote system will use to coordinate the exchange of data over a modem connection. Both systems involved in a file transfer must use the same protocol when exchanging files with one another.

▶ Computer viruses are designed to disrupt your PC operations. Although computer viruses are a real threat, most commercial information services and BBSs go to great lengths to avoid their spread. Anti-viral utilities provide additional protection against a virus infecting your PC.

Chapter 8

What's Out There?

In This Chapter

131

► *Computerized Bulletin Board Systems (BBSs)*
► *Dedicated E-mail systems*
► *Using your modem as an ersatz FAX machine*
► *PC-to-PC connections*
► *On-line research*

As I stated at the beginning of this book, your modem literally puts you in touch with the world, a world that encompasses much more than a few, preeminent commercial information services like CompuServe, Prodigy, and GEnie. This chapter explores several on-line alternatives to which a modem gives you easy access, as we examine additional options ranging from local electronic bulletin boards to dedicated research databases.

The BBS Phenomenon

Computerized bulletin board systems, or BBSs, best characterize the impact of modem communications. With nothing more than a personal computer, a modem, a single telephone line, and the right piece of software, anyone in the world can establish a centralized communications facility that, as little as a decade ago, would have required a mainframe computer and the resources of a major corporation to create and maintain.

The BBS phenomenon originated in the late 1970s, when a handful of computer hobbyists decided to share their interest in a miraculous new machine called the *personal computer (PC)*. Located in different areas of the country, these PC pioneers quickly realized that they had to come up with some means of providing a central clearinghouse for their discourse. The perfect tool ended up being the very technology that drew them together in the first place: the PC.

Stated simply, BBS software extends the basic functions of a communications program by endowing a PC with such useful capabilities as message storage and forwarding, unattended file transfer, and, in some cases, multiline access. (Many standard communications programs can run in Host mode, which provides some of these same features. We'll examine running communications software in Host mode in the next chapter.) Basically, a BBS operates in a manner very similar to commercial information services like CompuServe, only on a much smaller scale.

As a rule, individuals or groups of people collectively called *system operators* (or *sysops*) manage BBSs. The sysop is responsible for general maintenance chores such as verifying new callers, updating message bases, and managing uploaded files (including providing safeguards against computer viruses). Businesses, and even some government agencies, recently have started discovering the advantages inherent in electronic communication, even though individual users (the direct descendants of those early PC hobbyists) still run the majority of BBSs.

BBSs are usually organized around *Special Interest Groups*, or *SIGs* (electronic rooms where people gather to discuss their shared interests). SIGs are similar to the CompuServe forums or DELPHI groups, which we encountered in previous chapters. A given BBS, for example, might include several SIGs, each one dedicated to a different brand of personal computer: MS-DOS systems, Macintoshes, older Apple systems, Commodore computers, and so forth. Because of its capability to publicly post electronic messages, a BBS is often an ideal place to seek help for any problems you may be having with your PC equipment. Dial a local BBS that supports a SIG for your system type, leave a public message

132

describing your problem, go back on in a couple of days, and I can almost guarantee that you'll find more suggestions and advice from owners of similar systems than you'll know what to do with. System-specific SIGS also provide a convenient place to find public-domain programs and shareware designed for your PC.

Because of the way in which BBSs evolved, their emphasis on PC technology is natural. Over the past few years, however, many BBSs have expanded their SIG areas to cover a variety of noncomputer-related topics, everything from ideological and political discussions to new-age philosophy. In truth, calling a BBS greatly resembles taking part in an old-fashioned town meeting, where neighbors regularly meet at a central location and open the floor to virtually any subject.

After you feel comfortable using your modem, you might try calling one near you, just to see what the BBS phenomenon is all about. Appendix A of this book contains a representative listing of local BBSs, along with a telephone number and the appropriate modem settings for contacting each. Many sysops post listings of other boards, including ones in distant cities. Consequently, a single call to a local BBS can open an electronic door to a world of new on-line friends.

133

Dedicated E-mail Systems

In Chapter 6 we discussed using a commercial information service like CompuServe or GEnie for electronic messaging. A second alternative is to subscribe to a dedicated public E-mail system. The most popular E-mail services in the United States are MCI Mail, Western Union's EasyLink, and AT&T Mail, with MCI Mail claiming the largest subscriber base of the three.

> ► **Note:** In addition to the public E-mail offerings, many companies and organizations have established their own corporate E-mail services. These private E-mail systems restrict access to authorized users (generally company employees). However, in some cases this user base is expanded to include suppliers, vendors, customers, clients, and other external interests of the sponsoring company.

Because of the popularity of MCI Mail, I'll use it here to examine the kinds of services commonly available on a dedicated public E-mail system.

▶ *MCI Instant Letter.* The backbone of any E-mail system is its capability to deliver electronic messages with great speed. MCI Mail provides almost instant communication not only among its own subscribers, but also through special gateways, to several other popular on-line resources. For example, messages sent over MCI Mail get transferred to a CompuServe Mail address and picked up by the addressee on that commercial information service, usually within minutes of when it is written. MCI Mail also maintains links with Internet (a nation-wide, academic-oriented communications network), as well as several corporate E-mail systems.

▶ *MCI Overnight Letter.* This is the MCI Mail equivalent of an overnight delivery service like Federal Express. It allows you to have a printed message forwarded to an addressee by noon of the following business day, regardless of whether that person is an MCI Mail subscriber. By prior arrangement, MCI Mail will keep a copy of your company letterhead on file for use on any overnight letters you send.

▶ *The MCI Letter.* This option uses MCI Mail as a front end for the U.S. Postal Service, to speed up delivery of traditional mail. After MCI Letters are transmitted to a special MCI Print Center near the recipient's address, they are printed out on hard copy and delivered by First Class mail.

▶ *International Services.* Special letter and courier services are also available to deliver messages originating on MCI Mail to destinations outside the United States.

▶ *FAX and Telex Transmissions.* It's estimated that over 5 million FAX machines are currently in operation worldwide. Additionally, almost 2 million people subscribe to Telex services. Even if you don't own a FAX machine or subscribe to Telex yourself, you can use MCI Mail to communicate with other people who do. (The next section of this chapter contains more information on using your modem as an ersatz FAX machine.)

As you can see, even the basic services offered by a dedicated E-mail system like MCI Mail are impressive and all available at the touch of a few keyboard keys — provided, of course, that your PC hardware includes a modem. Appendix A of this book contains instructions on how to inquire about subscribing to MCI Mail, Western Union EasyLink, and AT&T Mail, along with a brief description of the rate structure of each.

134

The Fabulous "Faxing" Modem

Over the past few years, the *facsimile machine*, or *FAX*, has changed the way people do business in this country and around the world. Current FAX technology allows paper documents to pass back and forth over standard phone lines as quickly and as easily as a friendly voice-greeting. Today you don't even need a dedicated FAX machine to accomplish this. A simple modem will suffice.

Most dedicated E-mail systems and information services now provide a gateway to let their subscribers transmit FAX messages. This allows you to use a standard modem and your favorite communications program to send FAX messages from your PC. Transmission of FAX messages from someone else to you is more limited since it can't take place through a commercial service.

135

The E-mail/FAX Connection

Western Union's EasyLink, for example, lets you forward documents and even graphic images through a *FAX gateway* for delivery to any Group-III compatible FAX machine. EasyLink can handle any ASCII text document by automatically converting it to a FAX image before transmission. It can also transfer graphic images created in several popular formats, including PostScript, PCX, and TIFF files. If you send EasyLink a copy of your letterhead or even personnel signatures, the company will digitize them and keep them on file. By inserting a few simple codes into your ASCII document, you can automatically include these digitized images anywhere in the final FAX delivered by EasyLink.

The FAX transmittal is also offered by two other dedicated E-mail systems: *MailFax* (a service of AT&T Mail) and *Fax Dispatch* (a service of MCI Mail). Currently, MailFax can transmit graphic files only if you use AT&T's proprietary Access Plus software. MCI's Fax Dispatch accepts only ASCII files but, as mentioned in the previous section, allows you to register letterheads for inclusion in a FAX transmission.

Commercial Alternatives

Recently, commercial information services have started jumping on the FAX bandwagon by including FAX transmissions in their increasing list of available features. Using CompuServe, for example, you can transmit FAX documents over CompuServe Mail by simply adding a

>FAX command and the appropriate telephone number to the information normally entered at the To prompt, using the following format:

```
MiniCorp >FAX 212-555-1234
```

By combining the >FAX prefix with a destination address (in this case, an imaginary telephone number for a FAX machine at MiniCorp), CompuServe will take the message, translate it into FAX format, and then dial the specified number for delivery to a Group-III compatible FAX machine.

Currently, CompuServe allows you to FAX only ASCII files or text messages composed on-line. Unlike EasyLink, it does not allow you to FAX graphic images or even include letterheads and signatures in your documents. However, CompuServe FAX messages are accompanied by a cover page. The service always reports back to you on whether or not your FAX was delivered successfully through a Mail message. Undelivered FAX messages return to your Mail address for further processing, at your discretion.

The Finances of FAX

Using a FAX gateway offered by either an E-mail carrier or a commercial information service is not cheap. EasyLink, for example, charges 55¢ for the first 1,250 characters of a text document, and 35¢ for each additional 1,250 characters. For graphic images, EasyLink levies charges based on transmission time; 55¢ for the first 30 seconds and 35¢ for each additional 30 seconds. The cost to use AT&T's MailFax for either text documents or graphic images is based exclusively on page count. The company charges 50¢ for the first half-page and 40¢ for each subsequent half-page. MCI's Fax Dispatch, which also bases its rates on page count, is slightly less expensive than using AT&T to "reach out and touch" a FAX machine: 50¢ for the first half-page and 30¢ for each additional half-page.

CompuServe comes in at the high end of the price spectrum for FAX gateways. Sending a FAX through CompuServe Mail will set you back 75¢ for the first 1000 characters and 25¢ for every 1000 characters after that.

Clearly, using a dedicated FAX machine, for which you pay only the price of a long-distance phone call, is more cost efficient than transmitting FAX from your PC through a commercial service. One major advantage of FAX messaging through an E-mail system or commercial information service, however, is that you don't need to learn how to use any special equipment. You simply run your normal communications software, as you would for any other on-line activity. Additionally, if you FAX infrequently, it will take a long time for what you pay to FAX from a modem to surpass the one-time cost of a dedicated FAX machine.

PC-to-PC Connections

Of course, you don't have to depend on a commercial information service or dedicated E-mail system to recognize the advantages inherent in modem communications. The same equipment that grants you easy access to a distant mainframe computer can establish a very personal, one-to-one connection with another PC. To some degree, this is precisely what happens whenever you use your PC to access a BBS. You don't need a special BBS program, however, to make a PC-to-PC connection possible. Virtually any communications program will suffice.

137

It is possible to "talk" over a PC-to-PC connection. You simply type in your conversation, just as you would when participating in a real-time conference on a commercial service or BBS. However, it is not very practical. Entering words from a keyboard is an extremely inefficient way to communicate. If you merely want to hop on the phone and gab with someone, a good, old-fashioned voice call would be more appropriate. (I hasten to add, however, that the ability to telecommunicate represents a logical alternative to millions of hearing- or speech-impaired individuals who undoubtedly find it difficult to communicate over a traditional telephone.) Nevertheless, what if you find yourself in a position where you need to quickly exchange a file with a friend or business associate? That may be the perfect time to set up a PC-to-PC connection, especially when you consider how easy it is to do so.

Making a Connection

Establishing a modem connection is not that different from placing a regular telephone call. In essence, one modem (the originating modem) dials the number for a second modem, as you might call a friend. The second modem, in turn, assumes responsibility for answering this call.

For this reason, one of two modes must be activated on each of the modems involved:

▶ Originate mode
▶ Answer mode

What's the difference? Without getting too technical, the modem running in Answer mode assumes responsibility for generating that high-pitched tone you hear (providing, of course, that your modem is equipped with a speaker) whenever you establish contact with a remote system. The modem set to Originate mode, usually the modem placing the call, responds to this tone with a carrier detect signal, thus completing the connection.

Setting both modems to Originate mode is comparable to you and a friend trying to call each other at the same time, in which case both of you would receive a busy signal. Conversely, setting both modems to Answer mode is like the two of you picking up your respective receivers, but neither of you actually placing the call. Under both conditions, the result would be the same: You couldn't get through to one another.

138

Newer modems and communications programs assume responsibility for determining the appropriate mode for each system. For example, telling your modem to answer incoming calls, either by issuing the appropriate Auto-Answer command from within a communications program or entering an ATS0=1 command directly to reset the 0 S-register, simultaneously switches it to Answer mode. Conversely, each time you use an AT Dial command (or, alternately, select an entry from a program's Dialing Directory) to place a call, your modem configures automatically to Originate mode. Consequently, you rarely have to worry about manually setting Originate or Answer mode on your modem.

> ▶ **Tip:** If this is not the case, you can always use the ATA command to force the modem that failed to detect the incoming call into Answer mode.

Check Parameters

As is true for other types of modem connections, the two systems involved in a PC-to-PC session must use the same communications parameters. For example, if the modem connected to the other PC configures at 2400, N, 8, 1 (i.e., 2400 baud, no parity, 8 data bits, and 1 stop bit) then those are the settings to specify for your communications program, prior to placing the call.

> ▶ **Tip:** If you don't know the precise settings used by the other PC, don't panic. As you'll see in a few moments, some quick thinking and minor modifications on your end of the connection can clear up any problems resulting from a parameter mismatch.

Placing a Call

Establishing a PC-to-PC connection is a simple, three-step process:

139

1. If you know what they are, set the communications parameters on your system to match those used by the remote PC.
2. Have the person you are calling set his modem to Auto-Answer mode, using either the appropriate command for his communications program or by entering an ATS0=1 command.
3. Use an ATDT or ATDP command, or your communications program's dialing directory, to dial the number for the remote system.

As a rule, performing these steps will put your system in touch with a communications program running on the remote PC. From there, you and the person at the other end of the connection will be able to easily coordinate your activities (communicating on-line, initiating file transfers, and the like) with one another.

Solving On-Line Problems

"As a rule" is a pretty tricky phrase. In some ways, setting up a direct PC-to-PC connection represents one of the most difficult tasks associated with modem connections. There aren't any standard modem settings or automated sign-on procedures to simplify matters. Consequently, you and the person you're contacting must coordinate your efforts, whenever possible. Given this fact, problems can (and sometimes will) arise.

So, what kinds of difficulties might you expect to encounter when attempting to establish a PC-to-PC connection? How would you resolve them, if necessary? To answer these questions, let's look at an atypical PC-to-PC session. In this session, I've introduced several potential pitfalls and outlined the appropriate procedures to overcome each.

To begin with, I've set up two of my own systems to communicate with one another. All screens appearing in the following exercise are products of a Toshiba T3100SX laptop (the system that placed the call) using a 1200-baud modem.

The first time I tried to place this call, I looked up at the screen and noticed that all my keyboard entries were appearing twice on the display, as shown in Figure 8.1. The appearance of double-typed entries indicates an inappropriate *duplex setting*. The simplest way to correct this problem is to issue the appropriate Duplex Toggle command (sometimes called an Echo command) for your software. With Procomm Plus, for example, you accomplish this by using an Alt-E command to switch from half- to full-duplex.

140

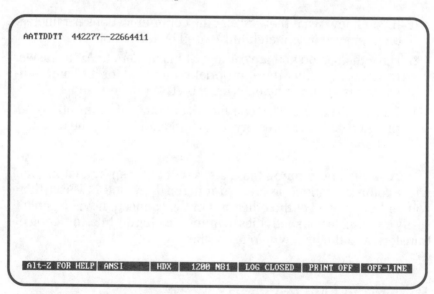

Figure 8.1 The appearance of double letters on your display indicates an incorrect duplex setting.

After switching to a full-duplex setting, I used the standard ATDT command to call my other PC, which I temporarily connected to my business phone. Once the connection was made, I decided to begin things on a congenial note and type in a short greeting. All I received back, however, was a line of garbage, as shown in Figure 8.2. (This same problem surfaced on the other system, as well. And, indeed, it did.) As a rule, garbage characters indicate that the communications parameters set for both machines are not the same.

> ▶ **Note:** Other programs may use different procedures to alter the duplex setting. If all else fails, manually change the duplex setting on your modem with an ATE0 or ATE1 command, used to turn Echo off and on, respectively.

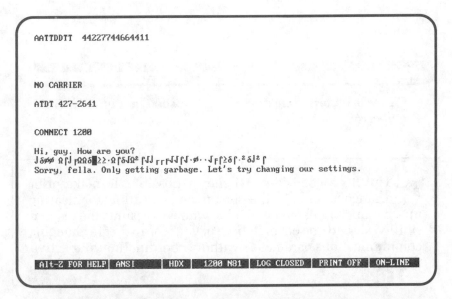

```
AATTDDTT  44227744664411



NO CARRIER

ATDT 427-2641


CONNECT 1200

Hi, guy. How are you?
♩δ♚♧ Ω∫J ƒΩΩδ█∑∑·Ω∫δ√Ω² ∫√J ᵣᵣ√√J√·∅··√ƒ∫²δ∫·² δJ² ∫
Sorry, fella. Only getting garbage. Let's try changing our settings.
```

```
 Alt-Z FOR HELP │ ANSI │   │ HDX │ 1200 N81 │ LOG CLOSED │ PRINT OFF │ ON-LINE
```

Figure 8.2 Garbage transmissions generally indicate a parameter mismatch.

This dilemma is slightly more difficult to correct than the previous error, given the variety of potential sources. Ironically, given how mismatched parameters totally disrupt communication, you and the person you're communicating with will not even be able to discuss the problem until after it's solved. As the Procomm Plus status line on the bottom of Figure 8.3 illustrates, the difficulties in this sample session cleared up when I switched to Even parity with a 7-bit data word and 1 stop bit (1200, E, 7, 1), an extremely generic modem configuration. A second likely candidate would have been to adjust the baud setting. It is also a common source of parameter mismatches in PC-to-PC connections.

Figure 8.3 Correcting a parameter mismatch is often a trial-and-error procedure.

> ▶ **Tip:** It's a good idea, whenever possible, to make prior arrangements with the person you are calling for clearing up a parameter mismatch. Decide who will assume the responsibility, should one occur. If both of you were to begin changing communications parameters without coordinating your activities, finding the correct combination would be doubly difficult.

Once you can communicate with one another, you and the person at the other end of the PC-to-PC connection can decide on a protocol you want to use and begin exchanging files, using the steps required by your respective communications programs. (See the previous chapter for more information on file-transfer protocols.) As was true with file transfers between your PC and a BBS or commercial information service, the file-transfer option you choose depends on the direction a file moves toward:

▶ If the file is being copied from your PC to the remote disk, commence uploading, while the person on the other end of the connection initiates downloading.

▶ If the file is being copied from the remote system to your PC, commence downloading, while the other person initiates uploading.

The ability to successfully set up a PC-to-PC connection and manage file transfers between the two systems involved can be a real life saver. Many times these connections have allowed me to meet tight deadlines by electronically delivering my columns, article assignments, even book manuscripts, directly to an editor's desk, using nothing more than my modem and Procomm Plus. Doing so is faster, more convenient, and cheaper than the alternatives.

On-Line Research

I still recall, with a touch of nostalgia, the 3-mile trek I was forced to undertake whenever a class assignment or other project from my high-school days demanded a visit to the local library for research. Today, in my role as a freelance writer, my assignment queue has increased enormously. Yet, I can't remember the last time I patronized a public library for more than a few moments to pick out a book or video tape.

143

Advantages of Electronic Research

Does this mean my acquired knowledge has reached a level where I no longer need to rely on outside resources? Hardly. (Believe it or not, I still have to look up my own telephone number from time to time.) Rather, it indicates a change in my personal research habits. I don't venture out into the world as frequently as I used to. One might say I've grown somewhat jaded as a result of having the world, quite literally, at my fingertips. However, this won't surprise anyone who has also discovered the advantages associated with on-line research. Consider:

▶ Of necessity, libraries maintain a somewhat restricted schedule. Most are open only 8 or 10 hours a day. By contrast, the vast majority of on-line databases can be accessed around-the-clock, 7 days a week.

▶ Even the largest library in a major metropolitan area can't possibly stockpile every shard of information to which its patrons may desire access. Smaller county and city branches often find that practical considerations (both physical and fiscal in nature) greatly limit the services they provide. The spectrum and scope of information available through various on-line databases, on the other hand, is virtually limitless.

▶ Information gathered during an on-line search can download to a disk file on your PC, making it immediately available for subsequent use.

▶ Finding information on-line is much faster and, once you master the appropriate search procedures for a given database, more convenient than hunting down that same information by cross-referencing card catalogues against books, newspapers, magazines, and other printed material (which is still required in a traditional library).

This final point brings up one of the more critical yet confusing aspects of using your modem as a research tool: finding information in an on-line database.

144

Database Searches

On-line databases contain a wealth of information. The secret is knowing how to track down the information you need. The larger and more diverse the database or research resource you access, the more critical these search procedures become.

With most on-line research resources, your quest begins when you select the database you want to access. DIALOG, for example, is arguably the oldest and most comprehensive on-line research system that can access more than 300 individual databases. In both structure and approach, DIALOG resembles a type of electronic clearinghouse. Specific databases available through DIALOG run the gamut from Agriculture to Zoology, and cover a wide range of topics in between. DIALOG assigns each database it supports a unique file number. The first step in a DIALOG search, therefore, is to specify the file number corresponding to the type of information you are looking for. (Of particular interest is File 411, DIALINDEX, which can help you identify the appropriate DIALOG database in which to start your search.) Once you're in a particular database, you can begin refining your inquiry even further.

In some cases, this involves nothing more than entering a key word that indicates the topic in which you're interested. For example, the key word `IBM` might be used to research the history of the IBM PC. Of course, such a general search would also turn up information about virtually every contribution that IBM has ever made to the computer industry — an almost endless list, I assure you. For this reason, many on-line databases allow you to construct complex search patterns based on Boolean logic, a search technique that uses comparative statements such as *less than*, *greater than*, *and*, and *or* to precisely identify the information in which you're interested. In the previous example, for instance, you might use the Boolean statement, `Find IBM and PC and Hardware`, to tell a database to seek only those records containing all three of the specified key words, thus limiting your research to IBM's contributions in the field of PC hardware.

The precise procedures and language used to initiate complex searches vary somewhat from system to system. Understanding the way in which search parameters work, however, can greatly increase the efficiency of all your on-line research activities.

145

Cost Considerations

Efficiency is critical to using an on-line database wisely. Electronic research isn't cheap. The cost of a DIALOG session, for example, ranges anywhere from 7¢ to $3.40 per minute. The cost depends on which database you use. A quick calculation reveals that spending as little as 10 minutes on-line with DIALOG can cost as much as $34.

At those prices, you'll want to sign on, find what you're looking for, and sign off as quickly as possible. Understanding how the system you're calling works, and planning your search strategy for a project will greatly reduce the cost of your on-line research.

An On-Line Sampler

There are literally hundreds of on-line research systems out there. Many are independent, dedicated databases. Others are accessed through commercial information services such as CompuServe or Prodigy. Some even straddle the fence. (EasyNet, for example, is both an independent research service and available as the IQuest option on CompuServe.) Listing all of them is beyond the scope of this book. A few, however, deserve mention.

The following list contains several of the more popular on-line research databases. I've included a brief description, address, and telephone number for each.

BRS (Bibliographic Retrieval Service)

Provides access to approximately 100 individual databases. Available topics range from business to medicine to the sciences.

BRS Information Technologies
1200 Route 7
Latham, New York 12110
(800)468-0908

DIALOG

Provides access to over 300 individual databases. Topics available include information on art, music, technology, books, economics, and hard sciences, among others.

Dialog Information Services, Inc.
3640 Hillview Avenue
Palo Alto, California 94303
(800)334-2564

Dow Jones News/Retrieval

Specializes in business-oriented news and information.

Dow Jones & Company, Inc.
P.O. Box 300
Princeton, New Jersey 08543-0030
(800)522-3567

EasyNet

General-interest databases covering a wide range of topics.

Telebase Systems, Inc.
763 W. Lancaster Avenue
Bryn Mawr, Pennsylvania 19010
(800)421-7616

Lexis/Nexis

Two databases from the same company. Lexis is a legal-research service. Nexis, a general-interest and business-news service, provides access to more than 650 news sources.

Mead Data Central
P.O. Box 933
Dayton, Ohio 45401
(800)227-4908

U.S. Naval Institute Military Database

Government-run information service specializing in military research.

United States Naval Institute
Annapolis, Maryland 21402-5035
(301) 261-2700

VU/Text

147

Central electronic clearinghouse for a variety of news services, magazines, and other printed periodicals.

VU/Text Information Services, Inc.
325 Chestnut Street, Suite 1300
Philadelphia, Pennsylvania 19106
(800)323-2940

Used wisely, a modem can be a highly effective research tool. You may want to check out a few of the services listed above, to see just how practical and convenient on-line research can be. As you noticed, most of them provide 800 numbers for user inquiries. A few calls (free) can put a world of information (quite literally) at your fingertips. That's a pretty wise investment, in anyone's book.

What You Have Learned

▶ BBSs, or electronic bulletin board systems, provide such useful features as special interest forums, message storage and forwarding, and unattended file transfer on a smaller scale than commercial information services. Individual users still run the majority of BBSs. Recently, however, a growing number of businesses and government agencies have started discovering the advantages inherent in electronic communication.

▶ Dedicated E-mail systems specialize in electronic messaging. These systems offer a wide range of services, including on-line communications, overnight message delivery, and even the forwarding of standard mail.

▶ Most dedicated E-mail systems and information services provide some sort of gateway that lets you use your standard modem and a communications program to initiate a FAX transmission. The types of FAX transmissions you can send from your PC vary from service to service. If you send out FAX messages infrequently, using an on-line service may be more cost effective than buying a dedicated FAX machine.

▶ A PC-to-PC connection provides an inexpensive, practical way to exchange files over great distances, using nothing more than a standard telephone line. When establishing PC-to-PC connections, both systems involved must be set up to use the same communications parameters.

▶ Using your modem to access an on-line database possesses several advantages over traditional research techniques. Because of the potential cost of on-line research, organizing how to search a database for information is critical.

Chapter 9

Where Do You Go From Here?

In This Chapter

149

▶ *Automating your on-line procedures*
▶ *Running your communications program in Host mode*
▶ *Remote access software*
▶ *Telecommuting*

The basics are behind us. You installed your own modem, used it to access several remote systems, and learned how to exchange information electronically over vast distances using E-mail, file transfers, and other common procedures. In this last chapter, we're going to touch upon some of the advanced aspects of modem communications. We'll begin by examining the different ways in which many communications programs allow you to automate your on-line activities.

Automating On-Line Activities

As I mentioned in Chapter 3, one of the features you should look for in a communications program is the ability to automate your on-line activities using a Dialing Directory or some other similar feature. If you're like most people, your modem communications will quickly establish a pattern. Chances are there will be certain services you contact on a regular basis. For example, I log on to both CompuServe and DELPHI several times a week just to check my messages.

Although I could manually sign on to these services each time I wanted to check my electronic mail, it makes more sense to let my communications program assume the responsibility. After all, the ability to automate repetitive tasks is one of the major benefits of using a personal computer. Why not extend this benefit to your on-line activities?

Most communications programs provide some method for automating your regular calls, often referred to as an *Auto-Dial feature*. Although the specific steps used to accomplish this vary greatly from program to program, the general procedures involved fall into two main categories:

► creating and maintaining some type of Dialing Directory
► setting up an individual parameter file for each frequently called remote system

Using a Dialing Directory

Procomm Plus, for example, allows you to automate the contact of remote systems with its Dialing Directory. Each entry in a Dialing Directory contains important information about the remote systems you call on a regular basis, including:

► the system's name or other identifying description
► the system's phone number
► the baud rate it uses to communicate
► the proper line settings (parity, data bits, and stop bits) for that system
► the correct Echo mode (full- or half-duplex) for that system
► an optional script file to run each time that system is called
► a default protocol for any file-transfers initiated while on-line with that system
► the type of terminal Procomm Plus should emulate whenever connected to that system

In addition to recording individual dialing entries for any computers you specify, the Procomm Plus Dialing Directory has several other
functions:

1. It sets Procomm Plus to Redial mode, where it automatically
   attempts repeated calls to one or more remote systems until it
   makes a connection with one of them.
2. It identifies and then begins to call multiple remote systems
   automatically.
3. It stores and uses up to ten special dialing codes. (Some connect procedures, such as accessing alternate long-distance
   carriers or dialing through an office PBX or switchboard equipment, require a dialing code in addition to the phone number.)
4. It switches between multiple directories, each capable of
   containing up to 200 listings.
5. It reveals information about the last time (and number of times)
   you called a remote system.

151

Figure 9.1 shows a Procomm Plus Dialing Directory that I created
to automate my on-line contacts. Notice how several of the settings
listed earlier specify each remote system in this sample directory.

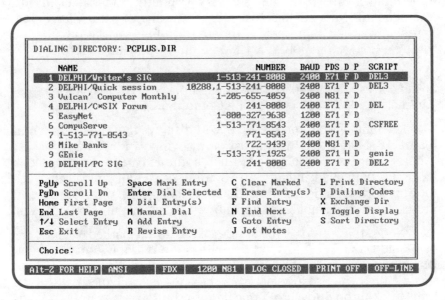

*Figure 9.1 The Procomm Plus Dialing Directory allows you to
automate calling the remote systems you use regularly.*

The Procomm Plus PCPLUS.DIR directory file (Figure 9.1) is empty when you first install Procomm Plus. This is, of course, as it should be. The primary function of a Dialing Directory is to reflect your personal on-line patterns. It took me several weeks, for example, to decide on the specific systems I wanted to include in my Procomm Plus Dialing Directory and then determine the most appropriate settings for each. (Astute readers have probably already noticed the entry in my Procomm Plus Dialing Directory for the Computer Monthly Electronic Edition in Figure 9.1.)

Setting Up Individual Access Files

Rather than use a Dialing Directory, other programs (such as MicroPhone II, a Windows-based communications package) have you set up individual procedures for each remote system you call. A familiar metaphor for this approach would be the Rolodex file many people use to keep track of important phone numbers.

Figure 9.2 shows a typical Windows display. (This particular screen was captured using Windows 3.0, the latest version of Windows released by Microsoft in 1990.) The title bar for the small window in the foreground of this screen identifies it as a program group associated with MicroPhone II. Notice that each icon (graphical image) in this MicroPhone II program group represents a different on-line service or program setting—CompuServe, BIX, MCI Mail, mini-BBS, and so forth.

Let's see what happens when we load one of these files by clicking on its corresponding icon. In this example, I'm going to look at the parameter settings associated with CompuServe.

Clicking on the CompuServe icon displays the screen shown in Figure 9.3. Notice that the title bar of this window now lists CIS.MDC (MicroPhone II's CompuServe settings) as the active file. It may not look like much happened, but in truth MicroPhone II configured itself to use the appropriate modem settings (baud rate, data structure, file-transfer protocol, etc.) for establishing an on-line connection with CompuServe.

Notice the buttons at the bottom of Figure 9.3 marked `On Line`, `Off Line`, and `Profile`. When working within the Windows environment, it's not unusual for application programs to include buttons similar to these, which you use to select from the options available at any given time. Clicking on the MicroPhone II Profile button, for example, allows you to specify CompuServe settings unique to your system and situation—such as the local access number, your user ID, and password—

using the dialog box shown in Figure 9.4. Entering this information would create an electronic analog of the Rolodex card mentioned earlier, one containing all the information MicroPhone needs to access CompuServe, using your local access number, personal user ID, and password.

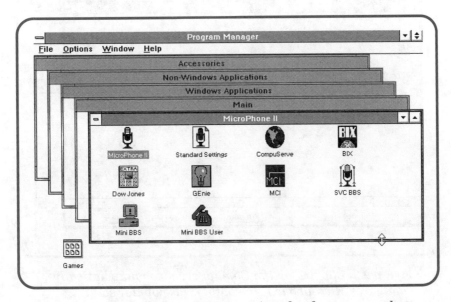

Figure 9.2 MicroPhone II is one example of a program that allows you to create a separate parameter file for each remote system you call.

Once again, the exact procedures used to create your access files will differ from program to program. It is important to remember that programs like MicroPhone II use individual files to automate the process of contacting frequently called remote systems, rather than the multiple directory listings created with a program like Procomm Plus.

Is There a Better Way?

Comparing these two techniques, you might ask yourself: Which one is better? That's entirely up to you. Like so many aspects of modem communications, the choice boils down to a matter of personal preference. Keep in mind that the *P* in PC stands for *personal*. Personally, I prefer the multiple-listing directories approach used by Procomm Plus. Something in my nature appreciates having a variety of choices from which to choose whenever I get the urge to go on-line. Other users I know favor the "one file/one service" approach supported by programs like MicroPhone II.

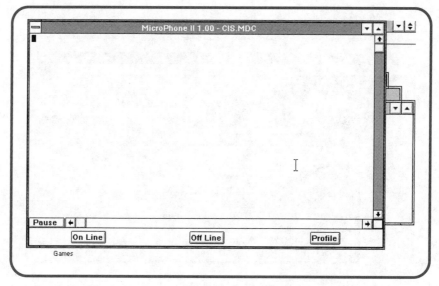

Figure 9.3 Clicking on the CompuServe icon automatically configures Microphone II to contact this popular service.

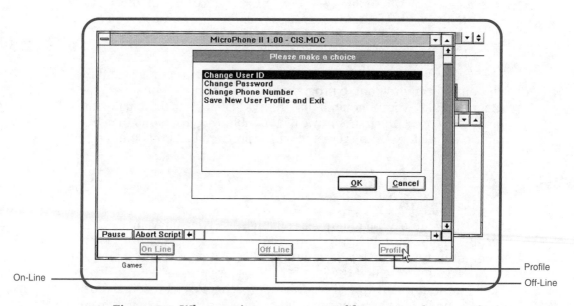

Figure 9.4 When setting up an access file, you need to specify those items unique to your operating environment.

Regardless of which method your communications program utilizes, it's to your advantage to become familiar with how this Auto-Dial feature works and use it. Pressing a few keys or clicking a mouse button is much easier and more efficient than individually setting your modem's parameters and manually placing a call each time you want to contact a remote system you access on a regular basis.

Scripts and Macros

A second, although more complicated, method of automating your on-line activities is to take advantage of a program's script or macro language, when one is available. If you have ever used a DOS batch file, you have a pretty good idea of what a script or macro is. It is a series of commands and procedures that executes automatically each time that script or macro runs. A script or macro can be as short and simple as a single command, or as long and complex as a given situation demands. Length and complexity, however, are the areas in which scripts excel, as compared to macros.

155

Although the two terms are often interchanged, many programs differentiate between macros and scripts. Both accomplish primarily the same thing; that is, they allow you to automate certain aspects of telecommunications.

Macros are used to reduce a relatively short command sequence to a single keystroke. You could, for example, create two simple macros to assign your user ID and password for a given system to a pair of keystrokes. Such macros would simplify initiating an on-line session. However, a macro supports only limited operations, as these two examples illustrate. You will find that many of the on-line activities that you'll want to automate will be much more complex than entering your user ID or password. Even more critical, they may be interactive in nature. For these situations, your communications program should be capable of responding differently to different conditions—something generally accomplished with a more powerful feature called a *script language*.

For example, many communications programs let you design a script that would automatically try calling a remote system. Should the first attempt fail, as might happen if all of its access lines were in use, the script would refer to its alternate set of instructions to disconnect from the current line. Then it would attempt to contact that service using some secondary access channel—perhaps a packet-switching network like Tymnet or SprintNet. Another way to use a script would be to automate the process of retrieving electronic messages from a commercial information service or E-mail system, a more complex activity than a normal macro can handle.

For example, using Procomm Plus allows me to write a script designed to call CompuServe, check if I have E-mail waiting, switch to the CompuServe Mail area if any messages exist (or, alternately, end the session immediately if my electronic mailbox is empty), transfer these messages to an archive file on my hard disk, and then sign off CompuServe and hangup the line. As a result, I can review this archive file, in much the same way I open and read the letters, magazines and, of course, junk mail—which is only now beginning to become a problem on-line—at my convenience. I could have even designed this script to begin execution at a specific time every day (late at night, for example, when connect charges may be less expensive) to automate retrieving electronic messages delivered to me over CompuServe Mail.

156

Look For a Learn Feature

Don't let that last section intimidate you. Phrases like *write a script* and *special instruction* may lead you to believe that creating a script requires programming skills. Nothing could be farther from the truth, primarily because most popular communications programs now offer assistance when the time comes to automate your on-line activities. Often called Learn, Auto-Record, or some similar name, this feature allows you to instruct your communications program to remember a series of commands and save them to a macro or script file.

Suppose, for example, that you want to create a script designed to automate a particular log-on sequence. To accomplish this, all you have to do is activate your program's Learn feature before manually placing your call. The software will keep a record of the individual keystrokes you enter while making the connection. The next time you call the same system, all you have to do is play back that recording and, voilà, instant access.

Figure 9.5 shows the pull-down menu used to automatically create a script using MicroPhone II. Selecting the Watch Me option from this menu tells MicroPhone II to keep a record of any keyboard commands you enter for the amount of time this feature is kept on.

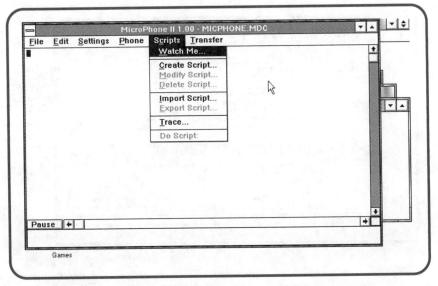

Figure 9.5 Many communications programs include an Auto-Record feature that allows you to record command sequences and save them to a script or macro.

157

For example, Figure 9.6 shows a script I created using MicroPhone II's Watch Me feature. This particular script modifies several of the program's default settings, including baud rate, terminal emulation, and file-transfer protocol. As I selected various options from the Settings menu, MicroPhone II automatically constructed the command sequence listed in the Watch Me dialog box to the right of this screen.

One step below automatically recording scripts is the process of creating them yourself by specifying the command sequence a given script should contain. Even at this point, however, your software may be able to help. For example, MicroPhone II has one of the most flexible scripting facilities I've ever seen. Figure 9.7 shows the MicroPhone II dialog box used to program scripts manually for that Windows-based communications program.

Notice the small box at the bottom left-hand corner of this dialog box. Each item in this box represents a specific activity you can perform with MicroPhone II. Instead of forcing you to learn the specific AT commands associated with a given procedure, however, MicroPhone II lets you identify that procedure by clicking on a simple description of the activity you wish to perform—Dial Service, Wait For Call, Hang Up, etc. (To access additional options, scroll down this list until it displays the desired operation.) Once you select a procedure, MicroPhone II assumes responsibility for translating it into the appropriate command sequence.

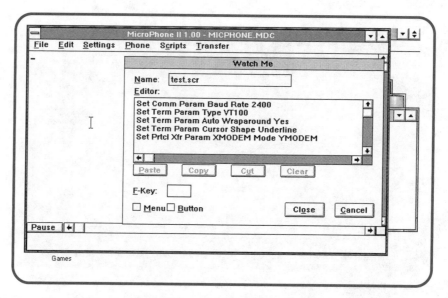

Figure 9.6 As you select options, the MicroPhone II Watch Me feature automatically converts them into the appropriate command sequence.

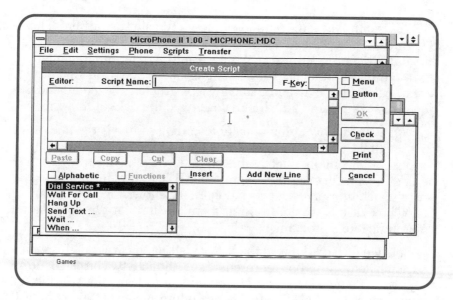

Figure 9.7 Some programs allow you to interactively specify the commands you want a script to contain.

As the previous examples demonstrate, taking advantage of a program's Dialing Directory, macro support, script language, and Auto-Record or Learn feature, if available, can greatly simplify telecommunications by allowing you to automate many of your on-line activities. If the communications program you use supports any of these features, I strongly recommend you familiarize yourself with how they work and then start using them.

Running a Communications Program in Host Mode

Have you ever been away from your home or office and discovered that you needed a file stored on your personal computer? When this happens, it doesn't really matter whether you're ten blocks or ten miles away. What you need is not where you need it. Setting up your communications software to run in Host mode can overcome this problem by allowing you—or anyone else with a PC, a modem, and an awareness of how this is done, for that matter—to access your system without your having to be there to accept the call.

I/O Redirection, the Secret Behind Host Mode

As a rule, Host mode works by redirecting selected *input* and *output* (I/O) operations on the Host PC to the COM port to which your modem is attached. In other words, when a communications program is running in Host mode, rather than sending its screen displays exclusively to the monitor of the Host system, it also transmits them through the modem and across the phone line to a remote PC. The same holds true for keyboard input. If a remote caller signed on to a computer running in Host mode requests a directory listing, for example, that listing will appear on his or her display screen, even though the files shown actually reside on your PC.

159

Host Mode Features

Depending on the specific features your communications program supports, running it in Host mode will enhance your modem operations to include one or more of the following capabilities:

▶ to upload files to and download files from the Host system

▶ to send messages to and receive messages from the Host system

▶ to execute program and, in some cases, DOS commands on the Host system from a remote location

Many communications programs provide additional capabilities in their Host Mode feature that will be of special interest to you, the person providing remote access to your PC. These include:

▶ determining how much freedom you want individual callers to have when accessing your PC from a remote location

▶ designating whether your PC is an *open* or *closed* system; that is, determining whether or not a remote session on your PC can be initiated by any caller, or only specified individuals

▶ creating customized log-on messages, which will be displayed each time a remote user calls your PC

Your Personal BBS

In essence, Host mode turns your personal computer into a scaled down electronic bulletin board system (BBS). For example, I use Procomm Plus running in Host mode as an informal, on-line messaging system. This allows selected clients, editors, friends, and fellow writers to exchange correspondence and/or files with me electronically, when I might otherwise be unavailable for such activities.

For example, if an editor has a question about an article or manuscript I'm working on and can't track me down at any of my normal haunts, the editor can simply fire up his or her own PC, dial my data line, sign on to my mini-BBS, and then use Procomm Plus's Leave Mail command to include that question in an electronic message. I can then review when I return home (or call in from a remote location myself) and check the sysop mailbox. The editor can even make the message private, meaning no one but the person to whom it is addressed (in this case, me) can access it. On rare occasions, I've even used Procomm Plus to let my family know where I am, what I'm doing, and when they can expect my return. (Because I am a writer, I work some pretty strange hours, especially when a particular assignment forces me on the road for an extended time.)

As you can see, while it is by no means as powerful or flexible as a full-blown BBS system, the Host Mode feature offered by many communications programs allows several useful operations to be performed on your PC from a remote location. And speaking of accessing your PC from a remote location, let's take a quick look at another type of program whose very name indicates that it was designed for precisely this purpose.

Remote Access Programs

How would you like to be working at home and still have access to all the applications and data files stored on your office PC? Or how about the possibility of traveling with a notebook computer that, by placing a simple phone call, could suddenly be endowed with all the computing power of a desktop PC? Sound too good to be true? Well, it's not. What makes all this possible is a relatively new category of software called *remote access programs*.

At the risk of sounding redundant, remote access programs allow one computer to connect with and control a second computer from a remote location. In essence, a remote access program gives you total and complete access to your system from afar. Using a remote access program lets you execute DOS commands and run application programs like Lotus 1-2-3 from a remote location. In other words, a remote access program allows you to work at a remote PC as if you were sitting right at its keyboard.

As a rule, a good remote access program includes the capability of transferring files easily between the two connected systems, a built-in phone directory, security features designed to guard against unauthorized access, session logging to record all Host connections, and a Chat mode that permits on-screen conversations between the remote user and anyone having access to the Host system.

Based on this list of features, your initial instinct might be to believe that using remote access software is not that different from running your normal communications program in Host mode. Both programs allow a person at one location to use a modem to call up and

161

take control of a second system at a different location. The real advantage of using a remote access program, however, lies in what happens after establishing remote connection. Whereas running a traditional communications program in Host mode limits you to electronic messaging and file transfer operations, a remote access program allows you to step outside the typical communications environment and actually run application programs on a PC being controlled from a remote location.

As a rule, you need at least two programs to initiate a remote session. The first, called a *control program* or *device driver*, is installed on the system you want to control from a remote location. The second, which you install on the remote computer, takes over and operates the other computer over a modem connection.

Some remote access programs demand that both packages be from the same manufacturer to communicate successfully with one another. Others are more flexible, and allow the remote computer to use virtually any commercial communications program. For example, PC Anywhere IV, a remote access program manufactured by Dynamic Microprocessor Associates, Inc., includes everything you need to set up remote access in a single package. By contrast, Close-Up, another popular remote access program from the Norton-Lambert Corporation, divides its remote and Host modules into two separate packages.

Remote access programs offer several advantages over the type of mini-BBS environment created by running standard communications software in Host mode. For example, as a computer consultant and freelance writer, I constantly have clients calling me with questions about or problems involving their PC operations. In the past, such calls almost always prompted an on-sight visit. However, using a remote access program, I can literally take over and run their system from my PC, as if I were sitting at its keyboard. In all but the most extreme cases, doing so allows me to diagnose the situation (and, in many cases, correct it) over a modem connection, without ever having to leave my own office. My clients also benefit, because their problems get resolved more quickly.

Although remote access is considered a fairly specialized branch of telecommunications, it's not for everyone. Nevertheless, the ability to use your modem to control a PC located elsewhere is not only technically impressive but, under the right conditions, it can prove invaluable.

Telecommuting

Perhaps the most critical aspect of telecommunications is not what it permits us to do now, but what a PC, modem, and the right software will allow us to accomplish in the future. The ability to link the world electronically guarantees eternal change. Harbingers of the changes to come are already surfacing—especially in the business community, where this new technology has been embraced with unprecedented enthusiasm.

It's estimated that approximately 20 million people living in the United States and Canada currently telecommute (use personal computers and modem-related technology to perform a portion or all of their duties in a location other than a traditional office). There is no verdict on what the full extent of the tangible effects of this movement toward telecommuting will have on productivity. Sociologically, however, its impact is undeniable.

Business has embraced the concept of a centralized workforce since the dawn of the industrial revolution. This concentration of resources has quite literally shaped our world, influencing everything from the creation and explosive growth of vast metropolitan areas to the planning and construction of the complex transportation channels required to connect them: rail lines, subways, highways, air transport systems, and the like. Over the years we perfected the process of moving people and things from one location to another, without considering the psychological and ecological consequences of our actions.

Realistically, a centralized workforce remains a requirement, when one is to manufacture and distribute physical products efficiently. However, move over to the services side of the economic equation, and the technical advances of the past decade alter the situation radically.

The concept of offices, corporate headquarters, service bureaus, and the like, evolved primarily from a need to concentrate information resources in a central location. Recent technological advances have all but eliminated this need. Today, by using a PC and modem, I can access virtually any information stored in a mainframe computer from virtually anywhere in the world. It doesn't matter whether I'm 1000 feet or 1000 miles away. Some studies indicate that as much as 50% of the tasks currently performed in offices could just as easily be accomplished in smaller and less centralized locations (such as a satellite or home office). Using the tools of modern technology to move some of these tasks out of the traditional office setting, therefore, only makes sense.

163

Consider the advantages inherent in such an approach:

1. Every day millions of people waste millions of hours in trains and planes and on the highways, just traveling to and from their offices. However, if these people were telecommuting, that wasted time could be spent working, an obvious and immediate benefit to everyone involved.

2. The impact of traditional commuting extends far beyond wasted time. Arguably, automobiles and, by extension, buses, trains, planes, taxicabs, and the like are the single greatest contributor to the pollution problems that plague our cities. Every time a company allows one of its employees to telecommute, that company helps reduce the number of vehicles that, both figuratively and literally, choke our highways during the morning and evening rush hours.

3. As any comptroller will confirm, keeping up a centralized workplace is exorbitantly expensive and extremely wasteful. Think about it. The average office building stands vacant almost two-thirds of the time. And yet, it must constantly be maintained; heated in the winter, cooled in the summer, cleaned, lighted, kept secure, and so forth. How much of this expense could be eliminated if people were allowed to work either in smaller, more efficient satellite offices or, even more convenient, out of their own homes? For a large segment of the workforce, a PC, a modem, and a telephone line would make this not only possible, but preferable.

4. Employees also suffer the expense associated with working in a central office. Gasoline, parking, automobile upkeep, meals, child care for working parents; each of these items costs money. The employee's savings from eliminating such expenses would more than offset the cost of any equipment required to telecommute.

5. From the employee's perspective, telecommuting is also more convenient than working 40 hours per week in a centralized office. Consider the anxiety and stress associated with traditional commuting, all of which would be eliminated for people permitted to telecommute. Also worth contemplating is the effect an increase in telecommuting (and an associated decrease in highway travel) would have on the appalling number of traffic-related deaths this country endures every year.

Is all of this merely a writer's pipe dream? Hardly. Modern technology has moved telecommuting from the realm of science fiction to the reality of 20th-century life. It seems only appropriate, therefore, that I end this book where it began, way back in its introduction, with my dream of an electronically linked world—a world in which the collective information, knowledge, and wisdom of that world lies but a few keystrokes out of reach. The recent emergence and subsequent growth of modem communications makes such a world not only possible, but almost predestined. I hope this book has helped prepare you for the day my dream becomes a reality. If it has, the world's out there, waiting. Go get it.

Happy modeming!

165

Appendix A

An On-Line Resource

To use your PC and modem, you must be aware of the other computers that are available. More importantly, however, you must know how to contact them. This appendix provides such information—on at least some of the thousands of commercial on-line services and local BBSs available to you.

What's Here

The specific information included for a given system usually depends on the type of system it is.

For local BBSs, I've included their access number (including area code), the line settings to use when calling them, and, whenever appropriate, a brief description of the type of services a particular BBS offers.

In case you need to know more about a given commercial on-line service, this appendix also provides phone numbers for a variety of them. As a rule, when you place the call, you will establish a voice connection. That is, you will actually be put in touch with another living being—a polite person who will answer any questions you might have about the commercial service he or she represents. Of course, because these are commercial ventures, this person will also be a sales representative and know how to sign you up for that service, should you decide to do so.

These listings represent some of the resources you'll need to get up and running with your new modem and communications program. Have fun.

Commercial On-Line Services: A Sampler

168

Commercial on-line services come and go. Some have been around for years and are still going strong, others are new and untested, while others appeared for a short while and faded from sight—victims of the same market influences that govern any commercial endeavor. The on-line services I listed in this book were seemingly healthy, profitable, and active when I completed this book. However, if some have since "gone under," or new ones surfaced, then my list will be unavoidably incorrect. All I can do is extend an apology, before the fact, for any confusion and/or inconvenience these inaccuracies may cause. These changes are inevitable in the dynamic world of telecommunications.

CompuServe

5000 Arlington Centre Blvd.
Columbus, OH 43220
(800)848-8199
In Ohio and Canada, (614)457-0802

Arguably, CompuServe is the most successful commercial service currently in business. In 1989, CompuServe absorbed The Source, one of the first on-line services to go into business. Until their recent merger, CompuServe was The Source's chief competitor. Consequently, CompuServe now claims over 600,000 subscribers, worldwide.

A partial listing of services CompuServe offers includes:

► electronic messaging and a variety of E-mail gateways through its CompuServe Mail service

► easy access to several commercial databases for on-line research

► an Electronic Shopping Mall

► the capability of uploading and downloading public-domain software and shareware for numerous types of personal computers and operating systems

► real-time conferencing

► dozens of user forums dedicated to such areas of special interest as comic books, gardening, science fiction, medicine, technology, and more.

Several manufacturers of PC hardware and software also offer on-line technical support through special CompuServe Forums. CompuServe also allows you to send and receive text-only (nongraphic) FAX messages, using CompuServe Mail.

169

DELPHI

General Videotex Corporation
Three Blackstone Street
Cambridge, MA 02139
(800)544-4005
In Massachusetts, (617)491-3393

Like CompuServe, DELPHI offers a wide range of options, all available at reasonable rates. Unlike some commercial services, DELPHI does not charge an annual membership fee, so you only pay for the actual time you spend on-line. Recently, in addition to lowering its hourly access fee to $6 per hour, DELPHI introduced its 20/20 Advantage Plan, a special billing arrangement that allows you to spend your first 20 hours each month on-line for the minimal fee of $20 per month. Electronic mail, special interest groups (SIGs), support forums, research databases, and real-time conferences are only some of the services available on DELPHI. (If you subscribe to DELPHI, drop by the Writer's Conference some Thursday night around 9:30 p.m., EST. That's when a bunch of us "professional writers" get together to discuss matters pertaining to a writer's life and just generally have a good time. All visitors are welcome.)

For on-line access to DELPHI and subscription information about this service:

Set	*your modem to 300/1200/2400-baud, E,7,2*
Dial	*1-800-365-4636*

Once a connection is established,

Press   *Enter once or twice to "wake up" the DELPHI system*

At the User Name prompt,

Type   `JOINDELPHI`

Press   *Enter*

At the Password prompt,

170

Type   `SIGNUP`

Press   *Enter*

The option of whether or not to subscribe on-line to DELPHI is your choice. If you do and, for some reason, are dissatisfied with DELPHI, the company offers a money-back guarantee.

Dow Jones News/Retrieval

P.O. Box 300
Princeton, NJ 08543
(609)542-1511

If business is your game, then you should investigate Dow Jones. Dow Jones, the mainstay of the *Wall Street Journal* financial section, also sponsors on-line commercial information service.

Needless to say, this particular offering has a business-oriented slant. For example, Dow Jones gives you fast access to up-to-the-minute stock quotes for both domestic and international exchanges 24 hours a day. It also includes several on-line reports, and in some cases, actual newspapers, ranging from Historic Dow Jones Averages to Standard & Poor's Online to excerpts from the *Wall Street Journal* to actual transcripts of the popular television show, "Wall Street Week."

Although Dow Jones is primarily targeted toward business applications, it is not exclusively so. It includes a shopping service, access to airline schedules, information on colleges and universities, movie and book reviews, and several other, less corporate activities.

BYTE Information Exchange (BIX)

One Phoenix Mill Lane
Peterborough, NH 03458
(800)227-2983
In New Hampshire, (603)924-7681

BYTE is a popular computer magazine. It has been published in one form or another for over 15 years. BIX is the on-line service sponsored by the same individuals responsible for *BYTE*. It provides a wealth of information on computer products and related technologies. You can, for example, submit questions to and get answers from regular contributors to *BYTE*. BIX also sponsors regular conferences on a wide range of computer-related topics. Beyond high technology, however, BIX also offers other services similar to those available from CompuServe and DELPHI—electronic mail, program libraries, vendor support, research databases, etc. I like BIX and sign on to it often, as will anyone who is seriously involved with computers.

171

Computer Monthly Electronic Edition (CMEE)

One Chase Corporation Drive, Suite 300
Birmingham, AL 35244
(205)988-9706

I used CMEE in various exercises throughout this book to give you some idea of how modem communications work. By now, therefore, you should be intimately familiar with this particular on-line service. Like BIX, CMEE is sponsored by a computer magazine, *Vulcan's Computer Monthly*. It, too, can be used to submit questions to and get answers from regular contributors to this popular publication (including me, since I write two monthly columns for it). CMEE doesn't charge an access fee for the time you spend on-line. People living outside the metropolitan Birmingham area, however, have to pay for a long-distance phone call when contacting this particular service. You can register directly with CMEE the first time you call that system, using one of the following access numbers:

1(205)655-4059 (2400-baud)
1(205)655-4065 (9600-baud or any slower baud rate)

Prodigy

445 Hamilton Avenue
White Plains, NY 10601
(800)776-3449 (1-800-PRODIGY)

In October 1988, IBM and Sears announced Prodigy, a joint venture designed to introduce the American consumer to Telex, a hybrid telecommunications/commercial concept that has enjoyed its popularity in parts of the European continent for several years. You cannot access Prodigy with a standard telecommunications program. Rather, it requires special software. The Prodigy access software is sold at computer stores, or you can order it directly from Prodigy by calling the number listed above.

Prodigy offers many of the same features as CompuServe and GEnie, including electronic messaging, on-line shopping, access to research databases, etc. Prodigy's unique twist, however, is that it also sells time to advertisers, in much the same way that a television or radio station does. As you use Prodigy, electronic commercials for these advertisers appear across the bottom of your display, like constant commercials superimposed over your favorite TV show.

The advantage to Prodigy's approach is that the additional revenue generated by this advertising allows the company to keep its access charges low, a flat fee of $12.95/month (at the time I'm writing this). The down side of this is that there's no way to turn off this advertising banner.

In its defense, I should point out that Prodigy's graphics-based user interface is much easier to navigate than the cryptic command menus used by most other on-line services. Consequently, it's a natural choice for the nontechnical neophyte just getting into modem communications.

172

GEnie

401 N. Washington St.
Rockville, MD 20850
(800)638-9636

If you think Prodigy is a deal, wait until you hear about GEnie. This popular commercial information service recently reduced its monthly fee to a mere $4.95, for unlimited non-prime-time access to over 100 selected products and services. With DELPHI, Prodigy, and GEnie now offering comprehensive access to their on-line offerings for a flat monthly fee, it appears that modem communications is starting to lean toward the same product/pricing structure used for years by cable TV companies.

GEnie offers the standard fare usually associated with a commercial service. Electronic messaging, real-time conferences, file transfer, on-line support for specific hardware and software products, electronic shopping, special interest round tables: all are available to GEnie subscribers. In addition, most are included in that $4.95 monthly fee.

173

Because GEnie still relies on text menus and an obscure command structure, it is not as easy to use as Prodigy. Nevertheless, GEnie's rock-bottom access fee makes it an attractive alternative for anyone wanting to test the waters of using a commercial on-line service. For a small investment you can learn a lot.

Electronic Mail Services

Electronic Mail (E-mail) operations resemble commercial on-line services in many ways. You sign on to an E-mail service much as you would CompuServe or DELPHI—that is, by entering your assigned user ID and password. However, they tend to focus on the types of services they support, concentrating primarily on offering an electronic analog of the U.S. Postal Service. Some E-mail services are accessed through commercial on-line services, and some allow you to access such services through special gateways. It's possible, for example, to send a message to someone's MCI Mail address from CompuServe's EasyPlex. They, in turn, can respond to your EasyPlex ID.

Businesses tend to like E-mail because it offers the immediacy of an overnight delivery service like Federal Express, at a fraction of the cost. One caveat to using E-mail is that, as a rule, they tend to be awkward (at best) when transmitting anything other than text files. At worst, certain E-mail services are simply incapable of handling other file types. You should consider this limitation before deciding on which E-mail service will meet your needs.

As was the case with commercial on-line services, the three companies profiled here do not represent a complete list of E-mail services.

AT&T Mail

P.O. Box 3503
New Brunswick, NJ 08903
(800)367-7225

174

AT&T Mail charges an annual fee of $30. In addition, you pay for each message sent, with this cost dependent upon message length. Like many E-mail services, AT&T offers an 800 number for actual connection, thus saving you long-distance charges to compose and deliver mail.

AT&T's MailFax lets you transmit FAX messages to anyone with a stand-alone FAX machine or, alternately, FAX capabilities on their PC. One big advantage in using MailFax is that you can FAX graphic files (if you purchased AT&T's proprietary Access Plus software).

MCI Mail

1150 17th Street NW, 8th Floor
Washington, DC 20036
(800)444-6245

Yes, the two biggest telephone companies are also squaring off against one another in the E-mail market. MCI's annual fee ($25) is slightly lower than AT&T's. Its per-character charge for sending messages, however, is slightly higher, at least for shorter messages. Basically, these two items cancel each other out.

MCI's FAX service, Fax Dispatch, is not currently set up to allow the transmission of graphic images. Fax Dispatch, however, lets you register a copy of your letterhead for a FAX transmission. MCI Mail's $10/month volume user's billing option is one of the better bargains available on any dedicated E-mail system. Like AT&T, MCI offers toll-free, 800-number access for its users.

Western Union EasyLink

1 Lake Street
Upper Saddle River, NJ 07458
(201)818-5000

With all the telegraph wires dismantled and Morse code messages mostly relegated to anachronism status, Western Union is attempting to re-establish its reputation in the communications industry by providing E-mail services. Whether it can compete with AT&T and MCI is a matter still open for discussion.

175

Perhaps the biggest disadvantage for EasyLink is its cost. Because it is not directly connected with a telephone company, the service eschews toll-free access. Consequently, in addition to its per-character delivery fees, which are lower than those charged by either AT&T or MCI, you must pay for the time you spend on-line, composing messages—at the rate of 15¢ per minute, as of this writing. Western Union also limits the amount of time unretrieved messages are stored on the system, unlike AT&T and MCI, who both provide an unlimited on-line storage period.

Western Union's EasyLink lets you forward text files and even graphic images through a FAX gateway for delivery to any Group-III compatible FAX machine. EasyLink can handle any ASCII text document, which it automatically converts to a FAX image before transmission. EasyLink can also transfer graphic images created in several popular formats, including PostScript, PCX, and TIFF files. One EasyLink feature of special interest to professional people is its capability of digitizing personal signatures and keeping them on file. By inserting a few simple codes into an ASCII document, you can automatically include these digitized images anywhere in the final FAX, delivered by EasyLink.

Local BBSs

These are the guys who really started it all. Long before CompuServe and years before AT&T ever got into E-mail, individual hackers started hooking up modems to their personal computers and providing an on-line forum for PC users to pursue their shared interests. If not for the thousands of worldwide, dedicated system operators back in the early days of personal computers, there might not even be a telecommunications software category. If there were, in all likelihood it would not be as prevalent, nor as profitable, as this type of software industry is today.

Your city, most likely, has one or maybe even several electronic bulletin boards located in or near it. To list all of these would be an impossible task, or at least a project beyond the scope of this book. (If you're interested, however, check *Vulcan's Computer Monthly*. It regularly contains a special section in which it publishes the connect numbers and access methods for hundreds of the BBSs located in various areas of the country. In fact, those listings helped me research the relatively sparse directory of BBSs I have included here.)

If the listings in my first two categories were incomplete, this one is positively bare-bones. Because of the sheer number of BBSs spread throughout the country, the best I can do is touch the highlights. I put them in alphabetical order by state, within the following compendium of several representative BBSs. Each listing contains that board's geographic location, a brief description of some of the services the board provides (in parentheses), its connect number, and specific information on that BBS's log-on protocols.

> ► **Note:** Although most BBSs provide free access (some sport a minimal registration fee to gain complete access to all their features), remember that the phone company will charge you for any long-distance calls you place using your PC and modem.

Like commercial information services, BBSs come and go. All I can guarantee, therefore, is that the following list was valid, as of December 1990, when I compiled it.

Alaska

Anchorage: Northern Lights BBS (SIGS, games, and shareware and public domain software for Amiga users), (907)337-4136, 300/1200/2400 baud, N-8-1.

Fairbanks: Help Yourself BBS (concentrates on IBM-PC, conferences and file areas and shareware product, but includes message areas for all system brands), (907)451-0887, 1200/2400 baud, N-8-1.

Alabama

Mobile: Computer Confabulation (6 conferences, 18 doors, messages, large selection of IBM software), (205)344-7606, 1200/2400/9600 baud, N-8-1.

Huntsville: Publisher's Paradise (specializes on issues relating to desktop publishing), (205)882-6886, 1200/2400/9600 baud, N-8-1.

177

Arkansas

Fort Smith: Data Plus BBS (specializes in IBM and clone systems, file transfers, games, conferences), (501)484-7821, 300/1200 baud, N-8-1.

Little Rock: CAPCUA BBS (support board for Central Arkansas PC User Association), (501)758-6045, 300/1200/2400 baud, N-8-1.

Arizona

Phoenix: JCCS BBS Node 1 (technology, science, current events), (602)582-3643, 300/1200/2400 baud, N-8-1.

Tucson: Old Pueblo BBS (MS-DOS systems), (602)744-2314, 300/1200/2400 baud, N-8-1.

California

San Jose: SERVU (MS-DOS, Macintosh, CP/M80, CP/M86), (408)238-9621, 300/1200/2400 baud, N-8-1.

San Francisco: Abacus RBBS (dedicated to Atari users), (415)587-8062, 300/1200/2400 baud, N-8-1.

Los Angeles: BBS West (Supported by UCLA PC Users Group), (213)473-2889, 300/1200/2400 baud, N-8-1.

Colorado

Denver: MICRO BBS (downloadable shareware and miscellaneous utilities for MS-DOS and CP/M systems), (303)752-2943, 300/1200/2400 baud, N-8-1.

Colorado Springs: Villa Hub (dedicated to TI99/4A and IBM computers), (719)574-2567, 300/1200/2400 baud, N-8-1.

Connecticut

West Hartford: University of Hartford BBS (Apple & IBM), (203)242-4738, 300/1200/2400 baud, N-8-1.

Brookfield: Wildside BBS (Echomail, DOS utilities, and programming information), (203)775-4627, 300/1200/2400 baud, N-8-1.

Delaware

Newark: FATHER Board (over 14,000 public domain files, also provides access to PC-SIG), (302)737-6041, 300 to 19,200 baud, N-8-1.

Florida

Miami Beach: Sunshine Online Service (Macintosh, MS-DOS, Apple, Commodore, Amiga), (305)378-6828, 300/1200/2400 baud, N-8-1.

Ft. Meyers: SWACKS BBS (sponsored by Southwest Florida Apple User's Group), (813)334-4259, 300/1200 baud, N-8-1.

Jacksonville: Galictic Infinutum BBS (all computer types), (904)346-3087, 300/1200 baud, N-8-1.

Georgia

Atlanta: IHBC BBS (information on running a home-based business) (404)482-5753, 1200/2400 baud, N-8-1.

Savannah: Savannah BBS (Supported by the Savannah PC User's Group), (912)920-2006, 300 to 14,400 baud, N-8-1.

Hawaii

Maui: Royal Hawaiian S/W BBS (group conferences and on-line entertainment), (808)857-5651, 1200/2400/4800 baud, N-8-1.

Illinois

Cahokin: Prolin BBS (aviation news, data libraries), (618)337-0162, 300/1200/2400 baud, N-8-1.

179

Decatur: U.S.S. Neversail (sponsored by the Commodore Computer Club), (217)877-8726, 1200 baud, N-8-1.

Indiana

Indianapolis: PC-DEN (MS-DOS systems, user help, Games, conferences), (317)862-5966, 300/1200/2400 baud, N-8-1.

Bloomington: Indiana On-Line (Accessible through Indiana Bell Public Data Network), (812)332-7227, 300/1200/2400/9600 baud, N-8-1.

Iowa

Cedar Rapids: Racing Greyhounds (for anyone interested in the greyhound industry), (319)362-7420, 300/1200/2400 baud, N-8-1.

Kansas

Wichita: Presipus BBS (all computer systems), (316)689-8771, 300/1200/2400 baud, N-8-1.

Kansas City: KCKCC (MS-DOS systems, over 300 files), (913)334-5511, 300/1200 baud, N-8-1.

Kentucky

Louisville: DISK (multiline UNIX system offering E-mail, multiplayer on-line games, and more), (502)968-5401, 300/1200 baud, N-8-1.

Lexington: Adventureland II (adventure games for most popular systems), (606)273-6252, 1200/2400 baud, N-8-1.

180

Louisiana

Natchitoches: Genesis BBS I (MS-DOS board with educational conference areas), (318)352-8311, 300/1200/2400 baud, N-8-1.

New Orleans: NOPCC RBBS (MS-DOS system sponsored by New Orleans PC User's Group and a FidoNet Node), (504)436-1825, 300/1200/2400 baud, N-8-1.

Maine

Brunswick: Baker Street BBS (Amiga user's board), (207)725-1417, 1200/2400 baud, N-8-1.

Maryland

Baltimore: Microline (private E-mail and over 20 sub-boards), (301)922-3843, 1200/2400 baud, N-8-1.

Massachusetts

Westfield: PVCC User Group BBS (sponsored by Pioneer Valley Computer Club, offers SIG doors to other systems), (413)568-4466, 300/1200/2400 baud, N-8-1.

Plymouth: Auto Exec BBS (specializes in database and programming issues), (508)833-0508, 300 to 38,400 baud, N-8-1.

Michigan

Detroit: Anchor BBS (sponsored by Michigan Commodore Users Group, Inc.), (313)293-7340, 300/1200/2400 baud, N-8-1.

East Lansing: The Program Exchange (large UNIX-like software library and message base), (517)332-0472, 300/1200/2400 baud, N-8-1.

181

Minnesota

Minneapolis: TCOS9UG BBS (sponsored by Twin Cities OS9 Users Group), (612)780-8936, 300/1200/2400 baud, N-8-1.

Mississippi

Jackson: MCS Micro Net (sponsored by Mississippi Computer Society), (601)992-4023, 300/1200/2400/9600 baud, N-8-1.

Missouri

St. Louis: SLACC STACK (E-mail, SIGS, shareware and public domain software), (314)367-1903, 300/1200/2400 baud, N-8-1.

Kansas City: COMP-SPEC (public domain files for MS-DOS systems and compatibles), (913)236-6530, 300/1200/2400 baud, N-8-1.

Montana

Dillon: Montana Gold West BBS (Montana tourist information and E-mail), (406)683-6285, 300/1200/2400 baud, N-8-1.

North Carolina

Asheville: Blue Ridge BBS (for IBM and Amiga users), (704)258-9017, 300/1200 baud, N-8-1.

North Dakota

Fargo: RBBS-PC of Fargo, Inc. (sponsored by Fargo IBM-PC Users Group; concentrates on law issues, Lotus, programming), (701)293-5973, 300/1200/2400/9600 baud, N-8-1.

Nebraska

Omaha: G.O.C.U.G. BBS (sponsored by Greater Omaha Commodore Users Group), 300/1200 baud, N-8-1.

Nevada

Las Vegas: Bytes BBS (sponsored by Las Vegas PC Users Group), (702)644-1157, 300/1200/2400 baud, N-8-1.

New Jersey

West Orange: SportsBoard BBS (technical and sports-related local and national conferences), (201)731-9425, 1200/2400/9600 baud, N-8-1.

New Hampshire

Bradford: Inter-active Micro BBS (downloadable files for IBM systems), (603)938-5230, 300/1200/2400 baud, N-8-1.

New York

New York: E.R.I.C. (technology, programming, buy/sell), (212)420-9380, 300/1200/2400 baud, N-8-1.

New York: Wise Byte BBS (programming, UNIX, Novel Networks, and more), (202)962-1946, 1200/2400/9600 baud, N-8-1.

Ohio

Cleveland: PC-Ohio BBS (sponsored by Greater Cleveland PC Users Group), (216)381-3320, 1200/2400/9600 baud, N-8-1.

Dayton: The Annex (games, doors, adult areas; callback connection), (513)274-0821, 300/1200/2400 baud, N-8-1.

Oregon

183

Portland: Portland PCC BBS (sponsored by Portland PC Users Group), (503)226-4142, 300/1200 baud, N-8-1.

Pennsylvania

Philadelphia: Chat Attack! (15-line multiuser chat and game board), (215)887-6600, 300/1200/2400 baud, N-8-1.

Harrisburg: BREC BBS (FidoNet node and FOG member), (717)657-8699, 300/1200/2400/9600 baud, N-8-1.

South Carolina

Hilton Head Island: Palmetto Software Exchange (technical games, utilities, messages, etc.) (803)671-9239, 1200/2400 baud, N-8-1.

Tennessee

Nashville: TANSTAAFL BBS (religion, philosophy, programming), (615)360-8419, 300/1200/2400 baud, N-8-1.

Virginia

Fairfax: REMJEM On-Line BBS (sponsored by Washington Area Commodore Users Group), (703)503-9410, 300/1200/2400 baud, N-8-1.

Texas

Dallas: Longhorn II BBS (sponsored by Dallas TI Home Computer Group), (214)240-4979, 300/1200/2400 baud, N-8-1.

Washington

Seattle: TIPS BBS (sponsored by Puget Sound 99ers), (206)784-4142, 300/1200 baud, N-8-1.

184

Wyoming

Casper: The Grasshopper Trap (sponsored by Casper Commodore Users Group), (307)577-7400, 300/1200 baud, N-8-1.

Appendix B

A Communications Software Sampler

This appendix will profile several of the more popular communications programs. For clarity's sake, it is divided into three different categories of communications software:

- ▶ standard communications packages
- ▶ remote access software
- ▶ additional options

> ▶ **Note:** The following profiles contain references to infor-
> mation presented throughout this book. If you find your-
> self unfamiliar with a procedure, term, or concept described in
> a specific profile, refer to the index to acquire additional details.

Standard Communications Packages

The packages profiled in this section represent full-featured communications programs. They are the types of programs used for the majority
of on-line activities.

Procomm Plus

Datastorm Technologies, Inc.
P.O. Box 1471
Columbia, MO 65205
(314)443-3282
Sugg. List Price: $119

As I've pointed out elsewhere in this book, Procomm Plus is the program I rely on for most of my on-line activities. I've been using Procomm Plus for almost as long as it's been available, and it has never disappointed me.

Procomm Plus originated as a shareware package called Procomm. In 1987, because so many people liked Procomm, Datastorm Technologies decided to release a commercial version called Procomm Plus. Since then, Datastorm has sold over 500,000 copies of Procomm Plus. Current estimates on the number of people who still use the original shareware version hover near the 1-million-plus mark.

The popularity of Procomm Plus is not surprising. It's an easy communications program to learn, intuitive to use, and it doesn't sacrifice strength for simplicity. The program's Dialing Directory, for example, allows you to automate your contact of up to 200 individual remote systems. Each entry recorded in the Dialing Directory contains important information about the systems you call, including its name or other identifying descriptions, its phone number, the baud rate it uses to communicate, its line settings (parity, data bits, and stop bits) whether it requires a full- or half-duplex echo setting, an optional script file you want to run each time that system is called, a default protocol for any file-transfers initialed while you're on-line with that system, and the type of terminal Procomm Plus should emulate whenever you're connected to it. Contacting a system recorded in the Dialing Directory is a simple matter of highlighting its entry and then pressing Enter. Procomm Plus takes care of everything else.

You can also use the Dialing Directory to set Procomm Plus to Automatic Dial mode, where it cycles through multiple directory listings until it succeeds in making a connection with one of them. The Dialing Directory also contains information about the last time (and number of times) you called the remote systems it contains.

Beyond the basic connection procedures initiated from the Dialing Directory, Procomm Plus's powerful Aspect Script Language can automate additional on-line activities, such as system sign-on, uploading and downloading E-mail, transferring files, etc. By attaching an Aspect script to a Dialing Directory entry, it's possible to transform virtually any on-line activity into a single-key operation. You can tell Procomm Plus to run scripts at a specified time. Consequently, you don't have to be sitting at your PC to contact a remote system. One practical use of this feature is to automatically initiate your on-line activities late at night (when telephone rates are low) while you sleep.

Procomm Plus has always supported extensive customization and configuration options, outstripping those available in communication programs costing several times its $119 list price. For example, you can select from 33 types of terminal emulation to contact a remote system, including several IBM, AT&T, Wyse, and DEC mainframe and mini-computer terminals. Similarly, Procomm Plus lets you choose from 15 standard protocols for file transfers. Popular protocols supported include XMODEM, YMODEM, KERMIT, ASCII, and COMPUSERVE B+, among others. Additionally, you can incorporate up to three proprietary options into your protocol list.

Procomm Plus allows you to use a mouse to initiate simple tasks such as accessing the program's pull-down menus, scrolling through incoming data, and viewing Procomm's multiscreen Help messages. Procomm Plus can be configured to take full advantage of any PC display standard, including several high-resolution VGA modes.

187

Especially impressive is Procomm Plus's Host feature. When Procomm Plus is running in Host mode, it transmits screen displays across the phone line to a remote PC, rather than sending them exclusively to your system monitor. The same holds true for keyboard input. If a distant caller requests a directory listing, for example, that listing will appear on his or her display screen, even though the files being shown actually reside on your PC. People calling into Procomm Plus running in Host mode can upload files to and download files from your PC to a remote system, send and receive electronic messages, and even execute DOS commands on your PC from the remote location.

Stated simply, running Procomm Plus in Host mode turns your PC into a scaled-down electronic bulletin board system (BBS). For example, I use Procomm Plus running in Host mode as an informal, on-line messaging system. This allows selected clients, editors, friends, and fellow writers to electronically exchange correspondence or files with me, even if I'm unavailable at the time.

For example, if my editor has a question about an article or manuscript I'm working on and can't find me, she can simply fire up her PC, dial my data line, and sign on to my mini-BBS. Once connected, the Procomm Plus Leave Mail command allows her to ask her question in an electronic message.

I also use Procomm Plus' Host mode to communicate with my family. Being a writer, I tend to work strange hours, especially when a particular assignment forces me on the road for an extended period of time. Leaving a message on Procomm Plus is certainly more convenient than awakening my wife at 3 or 4 o'clock in the morning. While certainly not as powerful as a full-blown BBS system, Procomm Plus' Host Mode feature is extremely impressive.

For only $119, Procomm Plus offers quite a lot. It is a powerful, flexible, yet easy-to-use communications program. And in today's market—where $400, $500, and even higher software prices are almost the norm—Procomm Plus represents one of the better bargains.

Microphone II

Software Ventures Corporation
2907 Claremont Avenue, Suite 220
Berkeley, CA 94705
(415)644-3232
Sugg. List Price: $295

As I've indicated several times throughout this book, the process of connecting your laptop to another computer over standard telephone lines can be a daunting task, indeed. Although it is a naturally complex activity, telecommunications is often made more difficult by poorly designed software. It's always a pleasant surprise, therefore, to discover a communications program that not only does what it's supposed to, but is also easy to learn and use. MicroPhone II, a Windows-based communications package from Software Ventures Corporation, is such a program.

MicroPhone II is like several other popular Windows programs (such as PageMaker and Excel), in that it originated on the Macintosh side of the PC fence. As a rule, programs that follow this pattern have most of the kinks worked out of them by the time they migrate over to the DOS marketplace. MicroPhone II is no exception to this general rule.

MicroPhone II simplified common on-line activities to such a degree that, within approximately 20 minutes of installing MicroPhone II on your system, you should feel comfortable using it. The credit for this should be divided equally between the Windows environment, which reduces most procedures to simple point-and-click operations, and MicroPhone II, which takes full advantage of Windows and then throws in a few additional conveniences of its own.

One of the best features of MicroPhone II is its script language. *Scripts* are preprogrammed sequences of commands used to automate many on-line activities, a real time-saver given the potentially high cost of telecommunications. Most communications programs include a Script feature, but MicroPhone II's has to rank among the most elegant I've seen.

Creating scripts with MicroPhone II is an almost totally automated procedure. To begin with, MicroPhone II includes a Learn feature, which is used to automatically record all the keystrokes and commands you enter during a given on-line session to a script for subsequent replay.

Creating scripts from scratch in MicroPhone II is also a breeze. While most communications programs force you to create and edit scripts with a Script editor—a procedure similar to using a programming language such as BASIC—MicroPhone II includes a special Script Construction module that allows you to interactively pick and choose the operations you want performed during execution of a given script. Although it wouldn't be appropriate to call this module intelligent, it certainly is intuitive and easily accessible—even to people who have never written a communications script.

When you select the MicroPhone II Create Script option, a special dialog box appears in your Windows workspace. This window is used to name your script, assign the script to a function key for automatic execution, and the like.

Microphone II also contains a Text Editing window, where you can begin entering the command you want executed each time this script is run. You might ask: What if I don't know the specific commands MicroPhone II uses for a certain procedure? No problem. You see, a second window in the Create Script dialog box contains a listing of all available MicroPhone II Script options—Dial A Service, Set Parameters, Send File, Receive File, Hangup A Line, and the like. By clicking on one of these options, you insert it into your script, using the appropriate command syntax. Furthermore, MicroPhone II automatically prompts you for any additional parameters a given command may require to execute properly.

Once a script exists, a special Check option analyzes it for any potential syntax errors that may render it unusable. There's also a Test option that allows you to interactively run a script, viewing both the script contents and the results on any commands it contains.

Finally, MicroPhone II comes with over 65 preprogrammed scripts to simplify everything from calling a specific on-line service to initiating a file transfer. Overall, I give MicroPhone II an A+ for simplicity, especially where its script language is concerned.

Like many communications programs, MicroPhone II includes a Host Mode feature. Put simply, setting MicroPhone II to Host mode causes it to automatically answer incoming calls and establish an on-line connection with authorized callers. Once this connection is made, the remote callers can use MicroPhone II to transfer files to and from the Host system, leave messages for other callers, or page and communicate with a user at the system running MicroPhone II.

If you're worried about security when MicroPhone II is operating in Host mode, don't be. Each caller must enter an assigned name and his or her personal password before MicroPhone II will complete the connections and grant access to the system. MicroPhone II also allows you to assign different security levels to different calls, a useful tool for limiting the operations a caller can perform once he or she is connected to your PC.

MicroPhone II comes with preprogrammed scripts for several popular commercial on-line information systems, including CompuServe, BIX, Dow Jones, MCI Mail, and GEnie. The first time you load a script for one of these services, clicking on a special Profile button causes MicroPhone II to display a series of prompts requesting the information it needs (such as access number, your user ID, your password, and the like) to connect you to that service. The Profile button can also change any of these items, as would be required, for example, if you moved and had to use a different access number to contact a given service. Again, simplicity seems to be the primary aspiration of MicroPhone II, a goal it achieves with ease.

For all its advantages, MicroPhone II has a few limitations. To begin with, it supports fewer file-transfer protocols than many other communications programs. Your options are limited to several XMODEM and YMODEM protocols, ASCII files transfers, and a standard binary protocol. However, one of the advantages of MicroPhone II is its ability to automatically determine the appropriate protocol for the Host system to which it is connected. Consequently, you don't need to specify this information, prior to installing a file transfer. Terminal emulation is similarly limited. Additionally, MicroPhone II does not currently support Dynamic Date Exchange (DDE), a special Windows feature that allows you to create dynamic links between multiple programs running in a Windows session.

Despite these minor shortcomings, MicroPhone II is a relatively powerful and, as I've stressed throughout this profile, impressively easy- to-use communications program—a rarity in the PC marketplace. If you need to open your Windows environment to the rest of the world, MicroPhone II is the logical choice for doing so. The fact that MicroPhone II is also available in a Macintosh version makes this the ideal choice for anyone whose PC setup includes the popular Apple system.

CrossTalk for Windows

Digital Communications Associates, Inc.
1000 Alderman Drive
Alpharetta, GA 30202
(800)241-4762
Sugg. List Price: $195.00

As more people discover Windows, more impressive graphics programs are beginning to surface. CrossTalk for Windows makes most of the features of its powerful sister-product, CrossTalk Mk.4, available to anyone who graduated from standard DOS to the Windows GUI. Furthermore, the procedures for using CrossTalk for Windows and for those incorporated into DOS resemble each other enough that switching from one to the other presents few problems. If you currently telecommunicate with CrossTalk Mk.4 or its sister-product, CrossTalk XVI, you should feel right at home using the Windows version.

191

CrossTalk for Windows supports most of the features found in any decent communications package. It includes a Dialing Directory to store vital information (such as phone number, line settings, and default file-transfer protocol) about any remote computers called on a regular basis. As an alternative, you can configure your hardware and CrossTalk for Windows "on the fly" (i.e., without accessing the Dialing Directory), then dial a number manually to connect with the unlisted remote systems in this directory. As expected from any Windows application, CrossTalk relies on a familiar Windows menu bar and subsequent option boxes to make performing these functions largely a point-and-click operation.

You may not expect the Windows interface to enhance telecommunications very much. If so, prepare to be pleasantly surprised. Specifying items like baud rate, parity, and data bits is greatly simplified when you can view various valid settings in an option box, and then click your mouse pointer on the appropriate selection. Another advantage CrossTalk for Windows has over text-based communications programs is reviewing data stored in the capture buffer, which is a simple matter of using the Windows scroll bars to replay previous portions of the current on-line session. You'll also appreciate the visual flexibility of a graphical interface, especially if you've ever faced the frustration of having your communications program overlay incoming data from a remote system with a message box or input prompt. With a simple drag of your mouse, CrossTalk for Windows lets you move the offending obstruction quickly and easily.

One advantage of telecommunicating with CrossTalk for Windows deserves special attention. Since it fully supports Dynamic Data Exchange, or DDE (a standard protocol used to transfer data between Windows applications), moving any information you capture from a remote system into another program for further processing is much simpler than, for example, the steps a non-Windows program forces you to go through to accomplish this same task.

192

Of course, Windows is not without its faults—faults that, in turn, are inherited by CrossTalk for Windows. Chief among these is that Windows recognizes only four serial ports, COM1 through COM4. This can be a real inconvenience if your Windows environment includes additional peripherals like a mouse (which is probably does), a scanner, a FAX board, and a laser printer. Be prepared to depend on A/B switches if you use several Windows applications. (Keep in mind, however, that this particular shortcoming is inherent to Windows, not CrossTalk.)

CrossTalk for Windows includes a pair of features that allow you to automate your telecommunications. To begin with, you can set up to 24 function-key macros for each listing in your Dialing Directory. When a listing is called, the macros assigned to that listing automatically become active. This provides a convenient method for keeping track of items like user IDs and passwords, which will differ for the various systems you call. Then, there's the CrossTalk for Windows Script Language, which resembles CASL (CrossTalk Application Script Language), one of the most popular features of CrossTalk Mk.4.

Stated simply, almost any CrossTalk for Windows operation can be automated with its script language, regardless of how complex it is. Scripts can be manually written to a script file, or recorded automatically using the program's Learn feature. (One caveat here: The CrossTalk for Windows Script Language differs slightly from standard CASL. Therefore, any CrossTalk Mk.4 scripts you currently use will, most likely, need to be tweaked before they can run properly under the Windows version.)

Of course, given that CrossTalk for Windows is a Windows application, you must have a version of Windows 3.0 running on your system before using it. However, once CrossTalk is installed (a simple operation accomplished with the program's Install program) you're virtually ready to go. Because Windows has already recorded important information about your hardware configuration, there's little additional work to do, beyond setting a few specific communications parameters (baud rate, COM port, modem type, and terminal emulation) with the CrossTalk Setup option.

Once CrossTalk for Windows is configured properly, learning to use it is a breeze. The program's well-organized User's Guide outlines all major program functions clearly and concisely, avoiding computer-ese in the process. After mastering the basics, a thick (both in size and subject matter) Programmer's Reference will provide a comprehensive resource for mastering CrossTalk for Windows' powerful script language—something you will want to do if your on-line activities extend much beyond an occasional call to a local BBS or commercial information service. In addition, remember that the on-line Help feature is always a mouse click away. To be honest though, using CrossTalk for Windows is more a matter of intuition than instruction, especially if you're already familiar with the Windows environment.

193

At $195, CrossTalk for Windows represents a complete and competitively priced communications program. It contains enough advanced features to handle all but the most demanding operations.

CrossTalk Communicator

Digital Communications Associates, Inc.
1000 Alderman Drive
Alpharetta, GA 30202
(800)241-4762
Sugg. List Price: $99.00

Responding to a changing software market, Digital Communications recently introduced CrossTalk Communicator, a scaled down version of its highly successful CrossTalk Mk.4 program. CrossTalk Communicator comes with 10 preconfigured Dialing Directory entries, including the proper procedures for calling CompuServe, Dow/Jones, and other equally popular commercial information services. If, however, you discover you need to set up your own directory entries to contact other on-line options, you will find the process very easy.

The program's file-transfer protocol options include COMPUSERVE B+, XMODEM, YMODEM, and ZMODEM, to name but a few. Communicator offers equally impressive options in terminal emulation. Included are DEC VT52 and VT100, ANSI, TTY, and IBM 3101, among others. Although its capability to create scripts is somewhat limited, Communicator will recognize and execute scripts written in CASL and supported by other members of the CrossTalk family of communications software.

Given the impressive nature of its price/performance curve, CrossTalk Communicator may be the perfect program for someone wanting to dip their toes into the waters of telecommunications. This program offers features way beyond its $99 list price.

BLAST

Communications Research Group
5615 Corporate Blvd.
Baton Rouge, LA 70808
(800)242-5278
Sugg. List Price: $250

BLAST deserves mention in any review of communications packages for one very special reason: It will run on more types of systems than any other communications program currently on the market. In addition to its excellent MS-DOS version, BLAST is available for computers that use UNIX, XENIX, VMS, or the Macintosh operating systems. Anyone with this program can communicate with any other BLAST user, regardless of the type of system he or she owns.

Variety is not the only spice in BLAST's life, however. The program includes a number of impressive features. For example, BLAST can be set up to emulate 13 different types of terminals, including DEC VT52, IBM 3101, ANSI, and TTY. If the specific terminal you need to emulate is not on the list, all is not lost. BLAST's keyboard remapping utility allows you to work around this problem by customizing your PC keyboard to a different configuration.

BLAST is no slouch in the area of file-transfer protocols, either. The standard protocols that it supports include XMODEM, YMODEM, and KERMIT, among others. A proprietary BLAST (Blocked Asynchronous Transmission) protocol even allows you to manually specify the size of a data block to optimize file-transfer speed, based on the quality of the phone circuit.

BLAST's script language (BLASTscript Programming Language) is easy to learn for anyone already familiar with standard BASIC, given the similarities between the two. If you're part of an organization that uses a variety of computers running under different operating systems, it's worth checking out BLAST.

Other Popular Titles

In truth, one could fill a book with comprehensive overviews of reputable communications programs. The previous profiles, however, should provide enough information for you to decide what type of program is best for you. In addition to the titles profiled above, I have provided an additional list of other popular titles, along with information on their list price and how to contact the company that manufactures them.

195

CrossTalk Mk.4

Digital Communications Associates, Inc.
1000 Alderman Drive
Alpharetta, GA 30202
(800)241-4762
Sugg. List Price: $295.00

DynaComm Asynchronous Edition

Future Soft Engineering, Inc.
1001 S. Dairy Ashford
Houston, TX 77077
(713)496-9400
Sugg. List Price: $295.00

HyperAccess/5

Hilgrave, Inc.
Genesis Centre
111 Conant Avenue, Suite A
Monroe, MI 48161
(800)826-2760
Sugg. List Price: $99.95 (DOS version)

Mirror III

SoftKlone
327 Office Plaza Drive, #100
Tallahassee, FL 32301
(800)634-8670
Sugg. List Price: $149

Professional YAM

Omen Technology, Inc.
P.O. Box 4681
Portland, OR 97208
(503)621-3406
Sugg. List Price: $139

QModem

196

The Forbin Project, Inc.
P.O. Box 702
Cedar Falls, IA 50613
(319)266-0543
Sugg. List Price: $30 (Shareware program)

Relay Gold

Microcom, Inc.
500 River Ridge Drive
Norwood, MA 02062
(800)822-8224
Sugg. List Price: $299

SmartCom Exec

Hayes Microcomputer Products, Inc.
P.O. Box 105203
Atlanta, GA 30348
(404)449-8791
Sugg. List Price: $129

WinComm

Synappsys
401 West Main Street, #300
Norman, OK 73069
(405)366-6363
Sugg. List Price: $149

Remote Access Software

This section profiles several remote access programs, which can be used to actually control a computer from a remote location. (See Chapter 9 for more information on remote access telecommunicating.)

Remote 2

Digital Communications Association, Inc.
1000 Holcomb Woods Parkway, Suite 440
Roswell, GA 30076
(404)998-3998
Sugg. List Price: $129 (R2Host module)
                   $195 (Complete package)

If you already own CrossTalk MK.4, CrossTalk XVI, or CrossTalk for Windows, you can begin reaping the benefits of remote computing for only $129. That's the stand-alone price of R2Host, the Remote 2 Host software. R2Host will also work with other communications programs, if they emulate one of several popular computer terminal types (DEC VT100, ADDS Viewpoint, Lear-Siegler ADM-3, and IBM 3161, among others). If you don't own such a communications program, a combined package containing both R2Host and R2Call (the remote module of Remote 2) is available for $195.

One area in which Remote 2 shines is security. You create a user table on the Host system to identify and assign passwords to authorized callers. Persons attempting remote access must enter the password assigned to their user name before access is granted. R2Host even lets you specify how many incorrect password attempts are permitted before the system drops the line and hangs up on a caller. A Callback function, where the Host system disconnects immediately following a successful sign-on and then calls back the remote user to initiate the actual remote access session, is also supported. Remote 2 even covers the possibility that a remote user might not always access the Host system from the same location. Entering a question mark in the Callback field of the user table instructs Remote 2 to prompt the caller for a number at which he or she can be reached.

When R2Call and R2Host are used together, Remote 2 attempts to eliminate line noise (a bad phone connection) with a proprietary error-correction protocol. This virtually guarantees a flawless link between the remote and host computers.

Both R2Host and R2Call let you keep track of remote sessions by maintaining an activity log. The Host log records each caller's user ID, along with the date, time, and duration of all remote accesses. It also keeps a record of any unsuccessful access attempts. R2Call maintains a log containing similar information on the remote computer for all outgoing calls.

Remote 2 is a practical package, dedicated more to function than form. Its screens, user prompts, and on-line instructions are minimalist in nature, but generally contain all the information you need to operate the program properly. If you already own a communications program that supports terminal emulation, at $129 Remote 2 represents the ideal introduction to remote computing.

PC Anywhere IV

Dynamic Microprocessor Association, Inc.
60 E. 42nd Street
New York, NY 10165
(212)687-7115
Sugg. List Price: $145

PC Anywhere IV includes two separate programs: the PC Anywhere Host software and Aterm, a proprietary communications package also from Dynamic Microprocessor Associates, Inc. Although the PC Anywhere Host software, like Remote 2, will work with virtually any communications software that supports terminal emulation, Aterm is specifically designed to enhance the program's overall performance.

PC Anywhere supports password protection, callback, and session logging. As an additional security feature, you can attach an automated script to a user's log-in procedure. You might, for example, limit a user to signing on to the Host system and downloading a specified file, after which you could preprogram PC Anywhere to drop the connection. When used in this manner, automated scripts give you total control over remote access to the Host computer.

If you use the PC Anywhere/Aterm combination, programs running on a Host system operate without a hitch on your remote computer. For text-based applications, transferring screen images between different video standards, (e.g., from an EGA-based host system to a CGA laptop) presents no problem. Graphics-intensive applications, however, are not as dependable. (In all fairness, though, this is a common problem with many remote access packages.) Beyond this one caveat, PC Anywhere should handle the vast majority of the activities (word processing, spreadsheet operations, database management, etc.) you'll want to perform remotely. At $145 for both the Host and remote software, it's the least expensive, complete remote access package currently on the market.

199

Carbon Copy Plus

Meridian Technology, Inc.
7 Corporate Park, Suite 100
Irvine, CA 92714
(714)261-1199
Sugg. List Price: $195

Even though Carbon Copy Plus' $195 retail price seems competitive with both Remote 2 and PC Anywhere III, it uses a serial number check to guarantee that each system involved in a remote access session uses a different copy of this program. This effectively increased the price of Carbon Copy Plus to $390.

Like Remote 2, Carbon Copy Plus uses a special table to list passwords and user IDs for remote users, as well as specify callback instructions, when appropriate, for each user ID. As an additional security feature, a special column (Password Options) in this table allows you to define different access levels for individual users. Carbon Copy Plus supports a comprehensive activity log.

One unique feature of Carbon Copy Plus is the program's built-in terminal emulation. When terminal emulation is specified, the remote module can access computers other than a Carbon Copy Plus Host (mainframes, information services, BBS systems, and the like) in much the same way you might use any powerful script language, which you can use to automate repetitive procedures such as initial sign-on, file transfers, remote printing, and others.

In terms of power, features, and system compatibility, Carbon Copy Plus definitely rates as the Cadillac of remote access programs. It's expensive, but you get what you pay for.

Close-Up

Norton-Lambert Corp.
P.O. Box 4085
Santa Anna, CA 93140
(805)964-6767
Sugg. List Price: $195 (Host module)
                 $245 (Remote module)

200

Perhaps Close-Up's best feature is its Automated Communications System (ACS), a powerful but easy script language that's integrated into the remote software. ACS allows you to preprogram a variety of tasks for the remote system. ACS scripts can be set up to run unattended at a preset time. This allows you to automate activities (such as file transfers between the Host and remote computers), while specifying that they be implemented late at night, when telephone rates are low.

Like Carbon Copy Plus, Close-Up supports extensive terminal emulation. It also has excellent security features, callback functions, and session logging. One useful security feature of Close-Up is that it allows you to disable the Host's display screen, keyboard, or both. This conceals potentially sensitive data from prying eyes, and helps ensure that a remote session will not be disrupted by curious hands.

For a single user interested only in having remote access to a home or office PC, Close-Up might be considered too much of a good thing. The $440 total price tag for both its Host and Remote modules will scare away many potential purchasers. However, if your remote access needs are more complex (e.g., you're part of a large company or organization in which several individuals must access and use a single Host system), Close-Up may be the perfect choice.

Additional Options

In some ways, I've saved the best news for last. Specifically, you may be able to test the waters of modem communications without having to buy any new software at all. That is, if you currently own or are thinking about owning one of the following popular operating environments or integrated packages, each of which includes a communications module.

Operating Environments

Microsoft Windows 3.0
Microsoft Corporation
One Microsoft Way
Redmond, WA 98037
(206)882-8080
Sugg. List Price: $149

GeoWorks Ensemble
GeoWorks
2150 Shattuck Avenue
Berkeley, CA 94705
(415)644-0883
Sugg. List Price: $199

DeskMate
Tandy Corporation
1500 One Tandy Center
Fort Worth, TX 76102
(817)390-3155
Sugg. List Price: $99

The DESQview Companions
Quarterdeck Office Systems
606-B Venice Boulevard
Venice, CA 90291
(213)314-3240
Sugg. List Price: $99

Integrated Packages

PC TOOLS
Central Point Software
15220 N.W. Greenbrier Pkwy., #200
Beaverton, OR 97006
(503)690-8090
Sugg. List Price: $149

PFS: First Choice
Spinnaker Software Corporation
One Kendall Square Cambridge, MA 02139
(617)494-1200
Sugg. List Price: $159

Microsoft Works
Microsoft Corporation
One Microsoft Way
Redmond, WA 98037
(206)882-8080
Sugg. List Price: $149

Framework XE
Ashton-Tate
20101 Hamilton Avenue
Torrance, CA 90509
(213)329-8000
Sugg. List Price: $149

SideKick 2.0
Borland International
1800 Green Hills Road
Scotts Valley, CA 95067
(408)438-5300
Sugg. List Price: $99.95

Lotus Symphony
Lotus Development Corporation
55 Cambridge Parkway
Cambridge, MA 02142
(617)577-8500
Sugg. List Price: $695

Appendix C

Troubleshooting Tips

Though loads of fun, telecommunications can also be very frustrating. When everything goes exactly as planned, you can spend hours electronically communicating with people from all over the world. Should something go wrong, however, an equal amount of time could be required to discover and correct the cause of your difficulties. In this appendix I'll explain some common complications that can arise during an on-line session.

Go to the Source

The first step in eliminating any problem is to determine its source. Successful telecommunications requires that several items work in tandem with one another. These items include your PC, modem, telecommunications software, and telephone system, as well as the various cables and connections that, quite literally, tie all these components together. A breakdown anywhere along the way, in any of these items, will close your digital doorway to the outside world. Where a specific problem originates often can be determined by analyzing how that problem manifests itself.

Suppose, for example, you attempt to dial a remote system and do not hear the tones that indicate your modem is placing this call. How would you find out where the problem lies? If you own an external modem, you could check to see if its status lights are lit. If they aren't you may be dealing with something as mundane as a loose or faulty power cord. If the cord checks out, then it's possible the modem needs replacing.

Cords and cables are another practical place to start when attempting to track down telecommunications-related problems. Even something as minor as the vibrations caused by walking can work a cord loose, over time. A quick check to guarantee that all your critical connections are in place can often get you back on-line with minimal effort. Speaking of cords and cables, here's a useful tip: If possible, set up your PC so that its various connections are easy to get to.

204   Not Just Any Port in the Storm

One common condition that can adversely affect your on-line activities is an improperly assigned COM port. Figuratively speaking a *COM port* (also called a *serial port*) is one of several electronic doorways that your modem and PC use to "talk" with one another. COM ports correspond to interrupt addresses reserved by your *BIOS* (*Basic Input/Output System*) to handle signals traveling back and forth between your PC and any one of several external components—a mouse, a printer, a scanner, a modem, and so forth.

If your communications program fails to work immediately following installation, it is probably because your modem and software are not configured to use the same COM port. If your system already has a mouse plugged in to COM1, for example, you may be forced to connect your modem to COM2, its second serial port. Most communications programs, on the other hand, ship with the first serial port (COM1) specified as their default communications port. Changing the default setting for your communications software from COM1 to COM2 will eliminate this problem.

A more difficult challenge is uncovering and correcting a conflict between your communications software and another application that may be trying to access the COM port it utilizes (sometimes without your even knowing it). This is the likely cause if a problem surfaces only intermittently—for example, should your modem periodically stop working in the middle of an on-line session. Should such a conflict exist, the signals being sent concurrently to two different devices by two separate programs through a single electronic door would run into one another, so to speak. Thus, preventing either of them from successfully reaching their final destination.

As I said, it's not always easy to ascertain the specific source of a conflict of this type. You may have a paint program, for example, that reserves COM1 for a scanner, even though your system does not include one. If you run that application before starting your telecommunications software, and it also uses COM1 for your modem connection, a conflict could potentially occur at some point during an on-line session.

Unfortunately, about the only way to eliminate this potential problem is to perform a comprehensive analysis of the manner in which the software you use most frequently configures your system, making sure no two of them attempt to access the same COM port.

Know Thy System

Of course, for your communications software to access a COM port successfully, DOS must be aware that that port exists. As a rule, DOS automatically recognizes and initializes any COM ports connected to your PC during system startup. What happens, however, if the expansion card containing your serial port works itself loose within your system? You could use your PC for weeks and, if you never tried to access that serial port, you'd never know this.

Several utilities exist that can provide an overview of your PC equipment. Two popular examples of such utilities are North Utilities System Information (SI) program and PC Tools' System Info utility. Figure C.1 shows a Report screen generated by Norton's SI. In this figure, SI reports DOS recognizing that two serial ports are installed on my Toshiba 3100 laptop.

The GIGO Syndrome

You don't hear much about *GIGO* anymore. Way back when the PC revolution first started, GIGO was a popular buzz-phrase. It stood for *Garbage In, Garbage Out*. (Real technical stuff, this PC jargon, eh?) While you may not hear a lot about garbage these days, you may see it quite frequently when you first contact a new BBS or commercial service.

```
           Computer Name:  Toshiba 3100
        Operating System:  DOS 5.00
        Built-in BIOS dated:  Friday, September 29, 1989
           Main Processor:  Intel 80386           Serial Ports:  2
             Co-Processor:  None                Parallel Ports:  1
   Video Display Adapter:  Enhanced Graphics, 256 K-bytes
      Current Video Mode:  Text, 80 x 25 Color
   Available Disk Drives:  4, A: - D:

   DOS reports 640 K-bytes of memory:
       68 K-bytes used by DOS and resident programs
      572 K-bytes available for application programs
   A search for active memory finds:
      640 K-bytes main memory      (at hex 0000-A000)
       64 K-bytes display memory   (at hex B000-C000)
       32 K-bytes extra memory     (at hex C800-D000)
    2,592 K-bytes expanded memory
   ROM-BIOS Extensions are found at hex paragraphs: C000

     Computing Index (CI), relative to IBM/XT: 15.0
         Disk Index (DI), relative to IBM/XT: 2.7

   Performance Index (PI), relative to IBM/XT: 10.9

   C:\>
```

206

Figure C.1 You can use the Norton SI program to determine how many serial ports are installed on your PC.

As I've stated previously in this book, it's critical that both computers involved in an on-line session use the same communications parameters: baud rate, parity setting, word length, stop bits, and the like. The first time you call a remote system, you may not know which settings are appropriate. If your best guess proves incorrect, you'll be greeted by garbage characters (a string of gibberish) once this initial connection is established. As a rule, such garbage indicates that you need to adjust your program's parameter settings to match the remote system's.

Because the majority of the remote systems you contact will use a modem that automatically detects baud rate, a good place to start is by selecting one of the two most popular parameter sets: N,8,1 (no parity, 8-bit data words, and 1 stop bit) or E,7,2 (even parity, 7-bit data words, and two stop bits). Should the problem persist, try lowering the baud rate from your modem's maximum setting; although high-speed modems can adjust to slower transmission rates, the reverse is not true. If you still have trouble, the only remaining option is to experiment with the individual parity, word length and stop-bit settings. Keep in mind, though, that you only need to go through this digital dance once. After you know the appropriate parameters for a specific remote system, it's a simple matter to adjust your program settings *before* the next call.

Hold That Call

Call Waiting is another potential troublemaker I've touched upon elsewhere in this book. That innocuous beep that heralds an incoming call on lines equipped with this modern convenience can wreak havoc on an unprepared modem connection. The good news is that many telephone companies now allow you to temporarily defeat Call Waiting by preceding the number you are dialing with a special code, usually either *70 or #70. With rotary phones that lack the asterisk (*) and pound sign (#) keys (or, alternately, on older, pulse-dialing telephone systems), you may accomplish the same thing with the numeric sequence 1170. To see if Call Waiting can be defeated on your phone system, simply pick up your phone and try entering the codes listed above. If you hear a second dial tone after any of them, then your local system supports this feature.

If none of these codes work, you could try increasing your modem's "lost carrier to Hangup command" setting to a higher number, using the ATS10 command. To set this to 100 on a Hayes-compatible modem, for example, you would use an ATS10=100 command. If this works, see if there's some way to specify the command in an Initialization or Startup command, so that it's executed each time you start your communications software.

207

What's My Line

The first time I ever made a modem connection, I remember sitting and watching line after line of text pour in from the remote system. Actually, that's not quite true. To be honest, I sat and watched a single line keep redrawing itself on the top of my screen, a sight that quickly became boring. It took a short call to a friend to discover my problem was caused by an incorrect carriage return/line feed, or CR/LF setting.

Most communications programs can be set so that a line feed is inserted every time a carriage return comes across the connection. As a result, the problem of single-line display is resolved.

The opposite of the previous situation is when everything coming through your modem ends up double-spaced on your display. If this happens, telling your communications program not to insert a line feed with each carriage return should resolve the problem.

The Answer Man

A friend of mine once complained that whenever his computer was turned on, it automatically answered all incoming phone calls and greeted the person on the other end of the line with a deafening screech. This didn't surprise me, once I discovered that my friend's modem was set up to run in Auto-Answer mode (unless told to do otherwise by his communications software). Changing the position of a DIP switch on his modem eliminated the problem and prompted several friends we shared to write me grateful letters of appreciation for helping to preserve their hearing. It's nice to be appreciated.

It's easy to assume that the default settings to which manufacturers configure their modems are the best ones available. Unfortunately, this isn't always the case. Furthermore, even if they are initially set correctly, switches can change from their original position by the jostling that naturally occurs during shipping or installation. It's always a good idea, therefore to verify that the default settings of your modem's dip switches are the most appropriate for your PC environment. Some careful checking during installation can prevent a lot of frustration further down the line, if your modem ever starts acting strangely during an on-line session.

Can't Get the Hangup of It?

Let's discuss a dip switch that often causes problems following the initial installation of a modem. Many communications programs drop a phone connection by turning off the *Data Terminal Ready* (*DTR*) signal to a modem. This works fine, providing the modem is configured to respond to the DTR signal. Some modems, however, including several Hayes models, ship with the DTR switch set to ignore the DTR signal. The most obvious symptom of this mismatch is your modem not automatically hanging up when you end a call.

The easiest way to solve this problem is to see if your modem contains a DIP switch marked DTR, used to specify whether it should recognize or ignore the DTR signal. If you find a DTR switch, check to see whether it is configured to respond to the DTR signal. If not, change the setting. Even if you can't fix things at the modem end, all isn't lost. Check to see if your communications program allows you to transmit an AT Hangup command (ATHO), rather than merely drop the DTR signal, to force disconnection. Your modem may take a little longer to drop a line using this method, but it works.

One More Switch

A second DIP switch that can disrupt on-line sessions is the *Carrier Detect* (*CD*) switch. Normally, a modem will automatically detect that a carrier signal has been dropped and instruct your communications program to indicate that you're no longer connected to a remote system.

Some modems, however, ship with a CD switch set to force the Carrier Detect signal on at all times. When this is the case, your software responds as if it's still connected, even after the modem has hung up the line. Resetting the CD switch to reflect the actual condition of the Carrier Detect signal will clear up this problem. If your modem does not have an adjustable CD switch, it may be possible to tell your communications program to ignore the Carrier Detect signal and automatically show that a session has ended each time it issues a Hangup Command. The flaw in this approach is that if, for some reason, the Hangup command doesn't work properly, you could remain on-line and not know it.

The previous situations do not cover all the difficulties you may encounter when making a modem connection. They do, however, provide a few examples of some common problems associated with telecommunications. Knowing where these problems can originate and understanding some of the steps involved in eliminating them can prove invaluable if it's your on-line session that's degenerating into a garbled mess or, even worse, never getting started because of a communications failure between your PC and the remote system. Troubleshooting is rarely enjoyable, but solving a problem makes the effort worthwhile and can bring the fun back into your on-line activities.

209

A Sample On-Line Session

Since you have just spent the last nine chapters and three appendixes reading about how easy and enjoyable modem communications can be, you must be pretty anxious to experience the sensation. And that's just what we're going to do in this appendix. It's time you experienced what I've been talking about.

The best way to accomplish this is to let you "look over my shoulder," so to speak, as I access CompuServe (using Procomm Plus) and experiment with some of its features. Don't worry. I'll approach this sample session as if I were a new user, one relatively unfamiliar with what a commercial service or local BBS offers and how it works.

We'll begin after I sign on to CompuServe by dialing a local access number and entering my user ID and password—steps commonly used to contact a commercial service or BBS, as outlined in previous chapters of this book.

> ▶ **Tip:** If the modem or communications software you purchased includes a trial subscription to CompuServe, as many do, now might be a good time to take advantage of this offer. If you get the subscription, then you could enter and execute the commands and procedures it contains right along with me. The card, booklet, brochure, or whatever you received with your hardware or software should contain instructions on how to sign up for your trial CompuServe subscription, if one is available.

Electronic Greetings

Like many on-line services and local BBSs, CompuServe begins each session by displaying a screen containing information about features or services recently added to the system. Figure D.1 shows a typical opening screen from a CompuServe session.

```
    CompuServe Incorporated
      All Rights Reserved

You have Electronic Mail waiting.
GO RULES to read new Service Terms



What's New This Week

  1 CompuServe Mail Receipts Charges Reduced
  2 Dr. Ruth Column in HSX Databank
  3 Commodore Applications Forum Opens
  4 IBMNET Announces May Focus File
  5 Electronic Mall Adds Computer Merchants
  6 OAG Offers New Look and Free Tickets
  7 Grolier's Encyclopedia Updated
  8 Save in Computer Database Plus in May
  9 Gifts From The Mall's Spring Guide
    (Above Articles are Free)
 10 Online Today
 11 Specials/Contests Menu (Free)
!

 Alt-Z FOR HELP| ANSI    | FDX  | 2400 E71 | LOG CLOSED | PRINT OFF | ON-LINE
```

Figure D.1   A typical CompuServe sign-on screen.

On CompuServe, this information is presented in the form of an options menu. Finding out more information about one of the listed topics is a simple matter of selecting the option number associated with it. (For example, if you wanted more information about Dr. Ruth's on-line advice column, you would choose the second option in Figure D.1.) Some services also use their opening message screen to display information for the current caller, whom they identify by the user ID he or she entered. (Notice, for example, that Figure D.1 contains an announcement indicating that someone has sent E-mail to me since the last time I signed on to CompuServe.)

Accessing CompuServe's Top-Level Menu

For this sample session, we'll bypass these new features and go directly to CompuServe's Top-Level menu:

Type   `GO TOP`

Press   *Enter*

```
   8 Save in Computer Database Plus in May
   9 Gifts From The Mall's Spring Guide
     (Above Articles are Free)
  10 Online Today
  11 Specials/Contests Menu (Free)

!go top

CompuServe                    TOP

   1 Member Assistance (FREE)
   2 Find a Topic (FREE)
   3 Communications/Bulletin Bds.
   4 News/Weather/Sports
   5 Travel
   6 The Electronic MALL/Shopping
   7 Money Matters/Markets
   8 Entertainment/Games
   9 Hobbies/Lifestyles/Education
  10 Reference
  11 Computers/Technology
  12 Business/Other Interests

!
 Alt-Z FOR HELP | ANSI    | FDX | 2400 E71 | LOG CLOSED | PRINT OFF | ON-LINE
```

Figure D.2   CompuServe's Top-Level menu

213

▶ **Note:** Opening announcements are not always a part of the CompuServe sign-on routine; sometimes you're taken directly to the system's Top-Level menu. Should this happen when you call in, don't worry. If the GO TOP command is issued when the Top-Level menu is already displayed, CompuServe will simple redisplay the menu a second time.

    This displays an options menu listing the major services offered by CompuServe, as shown in Figure D.2. Once again, CompuServe serves as a good example of how most commercial services and BBSs operate, in that it provides users with on-screen menus, from which they can select whatever activity they want to perform next. Anyone wishing to make travel plans, for example, could do so by selecting the fifth option, Travel. Subsequent menus would ultimately direct them to the On-Line Airline Guide (OAG), a special CompuServe section used to make commercial airline reservations.

Getting Help

For new users who don't know how to access a specific CompuServe feature, on-line help is available in the form of two special areas containing information about various CompuServe operations.

As an added attraction, CompuServe offers this assistance free-of-charge. As the FREE message shown in parentheses after options 1 and 2 of Figure D.1 indicates, the service suspends normal access fees, while you're working within either of its on-line help areas.

▶ *To access CompuServe's Member Assistance option:*

Type   1

Press   *Enter*

Selecting the Member Assistance option displays the menu shown in Figure D.3. CompuServe's Member Assistance menu lists additional topics for which you can request on-line help.

Still working from the assumption that we're first-time callers, let's request some basic information on how to use CompuServe.

▶ *To select the Command Summary/How to Use option:*

Type   2

Press   *Enter*

Figure D.4 shows the COMMAND menus, which contains a listing of the different types of commands available on CompuServe—menus, control characters, commands for navigating that service, etc.

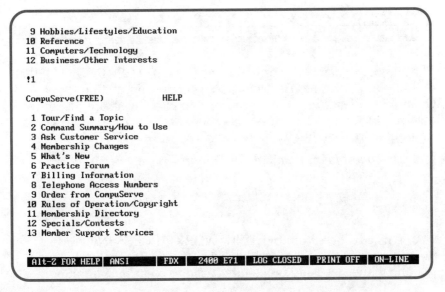

Figure D.3   CompuServe's Member Assistance menu.

215

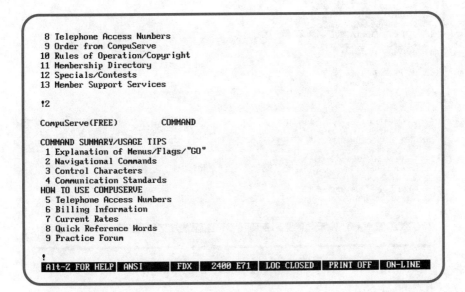

Figure D.4   The Command Summary/How to Use CompuServe menu.

Tracking Down an Access Number

The command menu also provides the HOW TO USE COMPUSERVE option, which can be used to access general information on various CompuServe features. The latter group of options, for example, contains a selection for looking up access numbers you can use to contact CompuServe from different locations.

▶ *To request information about CompuServe access numbers:*

Type   5

Press   *Enter*

This advances you to the NETWORK ACCESS INFORMATION menu shown in Figure D.5, which lists a number of on-line help topics relating to the steps and procedures used to contact CompuServe.

216

```
    1 Explanation of Menus/Flags/"GO"
    2 Navigational Commands
    3 Control Characters
    4 Communication Standards
HOW TO USE COMPUSERVE
    5 Telephone Access Numbers
    6 Billing Information
    7 Current Rates
    8 Quick Reference Words
    9 Practice Forum

!5

CompuServe(FREE)              LOG-1

NETWORK ACCESS INFORMATION

    1 Telephone Access Numbers
    2 Logon/Logoff Instructions
    3 Node Abbreviations
    4 Busy Signal/Network Problems
    5 Communication Surcharges

!
 Alt-Z FOR HELP| ANSI      | FDX | 2400 E71 | LOG CLOSED | PRINT OFF | ON-LINE
```

Figure D.5   The Network Access Information menu.

▶ *To look up the access number for a specific location:*

Type   1

Press   *Enter*

Selecting Option 1, Telephone Access Numbers, displays the menu shown in Figure D.6. You use this menu to identify the general location of the access number you want to look up. (Figure D.6 provides a hint as to just how popular CompuServe is. As this figure shows, it can be accessed from virtually anywhere in the world.)

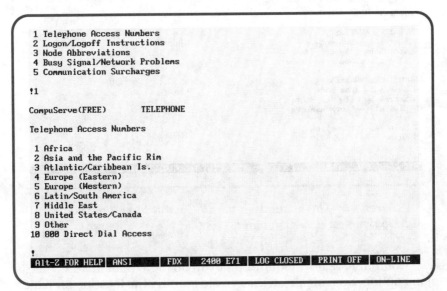

```
    1 Telephone Access Numbers
    2 Logon/Logoff Instructions
    3 Node Abbreviations
    4 Busy Signal/Network Problems
    5 Communication Surcharges

!1

CompuServe(FREE)        TELEPHONE

Telephone Access Numbers

    1 Africa
    2 Asia and the Pacific Rim
    3 Atlantic/Caribbean Is.
    4 Europe (Eastern)
    5 Europe (Western)
    6 Latin/South America
    7 Middle East
    8 United States/Canada
    9 Other
   10 800 Direct Dial Access

!
```

| Alt-Z FOR HELP | ANSI | | FDX | 2400 E71 | LOG CLOSED | PRINT OFF | ON-LINE |

Figure D.6   A CompuServe menu listing various international locations to choose from.

▶ *To look up a CompuServe access number in North America:*

Type   8

Press   *Enter*

As I pointed out earlier in this book, you may be able to call a specific on-line service using any one of several different methods. In addition to providing its own network of dedicated access numbers, for example, CompuServe can be contacted through a number of popular packet-switching networks (SprintNet, Tymnet, and so forth). You use the menu shown in Figure D.7 to tell CompuServe what numbers you want to see and the method you want to use to look them up.

▶ *To view all CompuServe access numbers located in a specific city:*

Type   5

Press   *Enter*

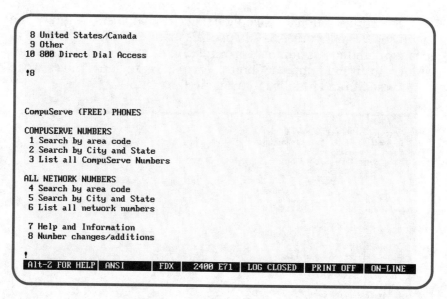

```
   8 United States/Canada
   9 Other
  10 800 Direct Dial Access

  !8



  CompuServe (FREE) PHONES

  COMPUSERVE NUMBERS
   1 Search by area code
   2 Search by City and State
   3 List all CompuServe Numbers

  ALL NETWORK NUMBERS
   4 Search by area code
   5 Search by City and State
   6 List all network numbers

   7 Help and Information
   8 Number changes/additions

  !
```
| Alt-Z FOR HELP | ANSI | FDX | 2400 E71 | LOG CLOSED | PRINT OFF | ON-LINE |

Figure D.7   The menu used to tell CompuServe how you want to look up an access number.

CompuServe now requires that you do more than merely select a menu option. Specifically, it asks you to identify the location for which you want to look up an access number. As Figure D.8 shows, the system itself provides an example of the correct format for entering this information, using Columbus, Ohio, the location of CompuServe's corporate headquarters, as an example.

▶ *For example, to request access numbers for Cincinnati, Ohio:*

Type   CINCINNATI, OH

Press   *Enter*

Next, CompuServe requests the baud rate you'll be using to contact it from this location. (Remember, most on-line services use different access numbers to support different baud rates.) To look up the Cincinnati number used to make a 2400-baud connection to CompuServe:

Type   2400

Press   *Enter*

What happens next is very much like what occurs when you use a commercial service for on-line research, a procedure discussed in Chapter 8. Based on the information (search criteria) you entered,

CompuServe scans a special file containing all of its local access numbers and displays any numbers it finds that match the specified location and baud rate. For example, Figure D.9 shows the local access number I requested (the 2400-baud CompuServe network number for Cincinnati, Ohio).

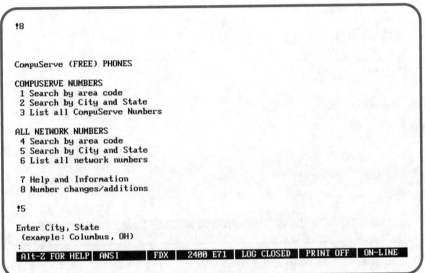

219

Figure D.8   Like many on-line services, CompuServe provides information on the proper method for responding to its on-screen prompts, when appropriate.

Braving the Bare System Prompt

At this point, CompuServe reveals one of its major shortcomings—a trait that, unfortunately, it shares with many other commercial services and BBSs. Although the vast majority of its on-line procedures are interactive (i.e., initiating them by selecting an option from a menu or using an obvious procedure), every once in a while CompuServe reverts to a bare-bones system prompt—often some type of brief message like Last page, accompanied by the totally uninformative exclamation point shown at the bottom of Figure D.9. (As I pointed out, however, CompuServe is not alone in its penchant for intermittent ambiguity.

Explore virtually any on-line service long enough, and sooner or later you'll discover its version of the infamous CompuServe exclamation point.) Naturally, you'll want to know what to do next...

```
   3 List all CompuServe Numbers

ALL NETWORK NUMBERS
   4 Search by area code
   5 Search by City and State
   6 List all network numbers

   7 Help and Information
   8 Number changes/additions

 !5

Enter City, State
 (example: Columbus, OH)
 : Cincinnati, OH
Enter Baud Rate: 2400

CompuServe (FREE) PHONES

City            State Net   AC   Access #
-----------------------------------------
Cincinnati       OH   CS M  513  771-8543

 !
```
| Alt-Z FOR HELP | ANSI | FDX | 2400 E71 | LOG CLOSED | PRINT OFF | ON-LINE |

Figure D.9   CompuServe finds the access numbers that match your search criteria.

Almost every on-line system has a special word or character it uses to manually initiate an operation (send an E-mail message, move to a different user area, or, as we want to do here, recall a menu) directly from the system prompt. On CompuServe, this magic word is GO, followed by the name associated with the menu you want to access. (CompuServe displays its menu names in capital letters, along with the menus with which they are associated. The options associated with Member Assistance, for example, are accessed from the HELP menu.)

▶ *To redisplay the Member Assistance Menu options:*

Type   GO HELP

Press   *Enter*

The GO HELP command returns you to the Member Assistance menu (Figure D.3). (Notice the uppercase word HELP located just above and to the right of this menu listing.)

Using the CompuServe Practice Forum

While experimenting with on-line help, let's examine another feature CompuServe provides. The Practice Forum, which can be accessed from the Member Assistance menu, allows you to become acquainted with one of the most popular activities on any commercial service or BBS: participation in SIGs (special interest groups) or, as they're called on CompuServe, Forums.

As explained in Chapter 8, SIGs and Forums are places where people can gather on-line to discuss their shared interests (from highly technical areas like biomedicine and computer sciences to more mundane topics like role-playing games and new-age philosophy).

> ▶ **Tip:** The GO FORUM command displays a menu containing the list of general subject areas in which CompuServe currently sponsors Forums.

221

▶ *To access CompuServe's Practice Forum:*

Type   6

Press   *Enter*

As the subsequent message screen in Figure D.10 explains, the Practice Forum is a "stripped down" version of a regular Forum. The Practice Forum will acquaint you with many Forum commands and procedures, without having to cough up CompuServe's standard connect charges.

I strongly recommend you spend some time in this Practice Forum before joining any regular CompuServe Forums. By experimenting with the various Forum commands in the Practice Forum, you'll feel more comfortable when you finally get out there "in the real world." In addition, you can play around in the Practice Forum to your heart's content, becoming a virtual on-line veteran, without spending a dime. (As I've pointed out several times throughout this book, telecommunicating is a potentially expensive activity. Why not save a little money by taking advantage of such complimentary offerings as CompuServe's Practice Forum, and increase your knowledge in the process?) For now, press *Enter* until the entire PRACTICE message is displayed and you return to the CompuServe system prompt (!).

```
!6

CompuServe            PRACTICE


One moment please...

Welcome to the CompuServe's Free Practice Forum!

As the name implies, this Forum is FREE of all standard CompuServe connect
charges.  However, please note that any communication surcharges are still in
effect.

This Forum is specially designed to assist new CompuServe subscribers in
learning and becoming familiar with the CompuServe Forum environment and
CompuServe's Forum command set.  Since this Forum is free of connect charges,
feel free to experiment and post any questions you have about using a
CompuServe Forum on this Forum's message board.

In order to participate in this Forum, you will need to select option 8 from
the main Forum menu or enter the JOIN command.  We encourage you to use your

Press <CR> for more :
Alt-Z FOR HELP  ANSI      FDX    2400 E71   LOG CLOSED   PRINT OFF   ON-LINE
```

222

Figure D.10   The Practice Forum is a logical place to begin
your examination of one of CompuServe's most popular features.

Looking Up Specific Commands

Here we are again, at that wonderfully cryptic exclamation point. We could simply use the GO HELP command to return to the Member Assistance menu. Instead, however, let's bypass menus for a moment and access CompuServe's Help features directly.

▶ *To display CompuServe Help options:*

Type   HELP

Press   *Enter*

Entering a HELP command by itself displays a brief message about how to use the CompuServe on-line Help system, along with a list of command words similar to the ones shown in Figure D.11.

> ▶ **Note:** As a result of CompuServe being a dynamic system, it undergoes constant change. Its features are continually improved, expanded, and refined. The Command list you see when you enter the HELP command may differ from the specific one shown here.

```
HELP, enter "..." (three periods without the quotes) at the next
prompt. The listing is long so remember to use CONTROL-S to pause
the output from scrolling and CONTROL-Q to resume viewing the output.
For general Forum information, enter the "INSTRUCTIONS" command at
the Forum menu/command prompt.

All Forum commands may be abbreviated to the first three letters of
the highlighted (capitalized) command word (i.e.  the COMPOSE command
may be entered as COM).

"HELP" may be entered at most Forum menus and command prompts to
receive specific help on a command.

More information is available for:

MESSAGES           LIBRARIES       CONFERENCE      ANNOUNCEMENTS
MEMBER DIRECTORY   OPTIONS         INSTRUCTIONS    JOIN
NEW                VERSION         WHO             EXIT
TIME               USTATUS         SEND            ULOG
HIGH               DESCRIPTIONS    NAMES           QUOTES
WEATHER

Enter HELP selection or
press <CR> to return to prompt:
```
| Alt-Z FOR HELP | ANSI | FDX | 2400 E71 | LOG CLOSED | PRINT OFF | ON-LINE |

Figure D.11   The CompuServe Command list.

Once you access CompuServe's on-line Help, you can request additional information about a specific command by entering that command when you see the following message:

```
Enter HELP selection or
Press <CR> to return to prompt:
```

> ▶ *For example, to request additional information about the WHO command:*

Type   WHO

Press   *Enter*

223

This displays the message screen shown in Figure D.12, which contains instructions on how the WHO command can be used in conjunction with a Forum member's user ID to request information about him or her.

```
MESSAGES          LIBRARIES        CONFERENCE        ANNOUNCEMENTS
MEMBER DIRECTORY  OPTIONS          INSTRUCTIONS      JOIN
NEW               VERSION          WHO               EXIT
TIME              USTATUS          SEND              ULOG
HIGH              DESCRIPTIONS     NAMES             QUOTES
WEATHER

Enter HELP selection or
press <CR> to return to prompt: who

Forum

 WHO

   Entering the WHO command at any Forum "!" command prompt will allow
   you to receive brief information about any Forum member.  After
   entering the WHO command, the Forum will prompt you to enter a User
   ID number.  Once you enter a valid User ID number, the Forum will
   tell you who that User ID number belongs to and the date and time of
   their last visit to the Forum.

Enter HELP selection or
press <CR> to return to prompt:
Alt-Z FOR HELP | ANSI     |    FDX |  2400 E71 |  LOG CLOSED | PRINT OFF | ON-LINE
```

Figure D.12 An on-line Help feature lets you request additional information about specific CompuServe procedures.

Using the EXIT Command

EXIT is another useful CompuServe command with which you should be familiar. Unlike GO, which takes you directly to a specified menu, EXIT is especially useful if you find yourself stuck at the system prompt, unclear about where you currently are (in the often confusing CompuServe menu structure) and uncertain of where you want to go next. As its name implies, EXIT exits the current operation and returns you to the menu from which it was selected.

For example, we began this latest group of exercises by selecting Practice Forum from the Member Assistance menu. To return to that menu:

Press   *Enter*

224

This will return you to the CompuServe prompt. (See the bottom of Figure D.12.)

Type   EXIT

Press   *Enter*

Violà! The EXIT command returns you to the Member Assistance menu. (See Figure D.3.)

Looking Up a User ID

As explained in the previous exercise, the WHO command allows you to look up information about other CompuServe subscribers, based on their user ID. To be honest, I've always considered that to be a little strange. After all, the WHO command doesn't help much if you don't know the person's user ID. Luckily, the Membership Directory option of the Member Assistance menu provides a convenient method for cross-referencing someone's user ID, using his or her last name.

225

 To look up the user ID of another subscriber:

Type   11

Press   *Enter*

As it did with the access numbers, CompuServe displays a list of options you can use to narrow down the scope of your search, as shown in Figure D.13. We'll limit our search to subscribers who live in North America.

 To find a user ID for a North American subscriber:

Type   2

Press   *Enter*

Next, you're asked to enter the last name of the subscriber you want to find. (See Figure D.14.) There's one person whose user ID I have memorized, so I'll use his name to test the Membership Directory option.

 To display the person's user ID:

Type   NIMERSHEIM

Press   *Enter*

```
 8 Telephone Access Numbers
 9 Order from CompuServe
10 Rules of Operation/Copyright
11 Membership Directory
12 Specials/Contests
13 Member Support Services

!11


One moment please...

CompuServe(FREE)        DIRECTORY

MEMBER DIRECTORY

 1 Explanation
 2 Member Directory Search
    (U.S. and Canada)
 3 Member Directory Search
    (International)
 4 Include/Exclude This User ID

!
Alt-Z FOR HELP | ANSI |    FDX |  2400 E71 | LOG CLOSED | PRINT OFF | ON-LINE
```

226

Figure D.13   The Membership Directory option.

```
12 Specials/Contests
13 Member Support Services

!11


One moment please...

CompuServe(FREE)        DIRECTORY

MEMBER DIRECTORY

 1 Explanation
 2 Member Directory Search
    (U.S. and Canada)
 3 Member Directory Search
    (International)
 4 Include/Exclude This User ID

!2


Last name (<CR> to exit):
Alt-Z FOR HELP | ANSI |    FDX |  2400 E71 | LOG CLOSED | PRINT OFF | ON-LINE
```

Figure D.14   The Membership Directory Last Name prompt.

Figure D.15 contains the result of this search. Trust me, the information shown is correct. I do live in a small Indiana town called Vevay, and that is my user ID. (Once you get more familiar with how

CompuServe works, feel free to send me an E-mail message, if you'd like. Despite our reclusive reputations, writers love to hear from their readers.)

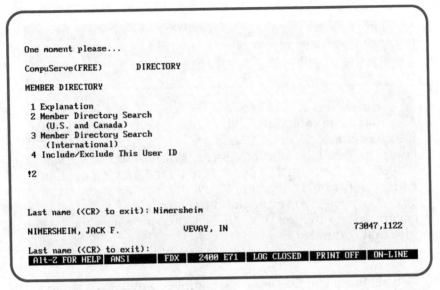

```
One moment please...

CompuServe(FREE)        DIRECTORY

MEMBER DIRECTORY

 1 Explanation
 2 Member Directory Search
    (U.S. and Canada)
 3 Member Directory Search
    (International)
 4 Include/Exclude This User ID

!2


Last name (<CR> to exit): Nimersheim

NIMERSHEIM, JACK F.          VEVAY, IN                    73047,1122

Last name (<CR> to exit):
Alt-Z FOR HELP| ANSI    |  FDX  | 2400 E71 | LOG CLOSED | PRINT OFF | ON-LINE
```

Figure D.15   If you know a subscriber's last name, it's easy to look up his or her user ID.

▶ *To exit the Membership Directory:*

Press   *Enter*

▶ *This will remove the Last Name prompt.*

Type   EXIT

Press   *Enter*

Signing Off CompuServe

The final CompuServe command we'll look at is one everybody uses: the BYE command. Stated simply, you use the BYE command to end the current on-line session and sign off CompuServe.

▶ *To end this sample session:*

Type   BYE

Press   *Enter*

There really isn't any more to it than that. When you issue the BYE command, CompuServe reports on how long your current session lasted and then drops you off the system.

▶ **Tip:** Depending on how you called in to CompuServe, you may need to manually disconnect your modem from an intermediate service, such as a packet-switching network, to completely end the current session. The easiest way to accomplish this is by using the Hangup command for your communications software. In Procomm Plus (the communications program I've been using throughout the previous exercises) this is accomplished by pressing Alt-H. Other programs may use a different command.

228

Well, that about does it for our sample CompuServe session. As I stated at the beginning of this appendix, my goal was not to transform you into an on-line expert. (CompuServe is an extremely powerful and complex commercial service. In fact, entire books have been written about its various features, forums, commands, options, procedures, and so forth.) All I wanted to do was help you feel comfortable interacting with a remote system. (Feel free to let me know how things are going. After all, you have my user ID.)

Glossary

analog signals. The type of tones normally transmitted over standard telephone lines. A modem converts the digital signals generated by your PC into analog tones during an on-line session.

ASCII. Acronym for American Standard Code for Information Interchange. ASCII is the most "vanilla" format available for storing text files. Basically, an ASCII file contains a series of numbers, each corresponding to access codes.

asynchronous. A communication method in which information exchange is coordinated by separating individual characters with start- and stop-bits, rather than using a prearranged, uniform time period to alternate data transmission between the two modems involved. Most PC-to-PC modem communications are asynchronous connections.

AT command set. A series of commands (first popularized by Hayes modems) used to manage telecommunications. This command set derives its name from the fact that you precede its commands (or instructions) with the letters "AT" to get the ATtention of your modem. The AT command set has evolved into a standard for PC telecommunications.

auto answer. The condition where your modem has been instructed to automatically answer any incoming calls and then generate a carrier tone to establish a connection with a remote computer.

baud rate. A measurement of the number of times a modem changes the frequency of its carrier signal. Though expressed as bits-per-second (bps), a modem's baud rate is not necessarily a true measurement of how fast data actually is transmitted during a communications session.

BBS. Abbreviation for Bulletin Board System. Appendix A of this book contains a partial listing of BBS systems located throughout the United States.

binary notation. A notation system that uses only two numbers. Computers rely on binary notation to indicate the status of their electronic switches, with 0 and 1 used to represent off or on, respectively.

bit. Contraction for binary digit. The smallest information unit identified by a computer.

block. A cluster of data transmitted as a single unit during a telecommunications session. Most file-transfer protocols break large files down into discrete blocks before transmission.

bps. Abbreviation for bits-per-second. This is the actual number of bits (binary digits) transferred every second during an on-line session. The bps measurement can differ from baud rate, since it often takes multiple state changes (baud) to transmit a single bit.

buffer. A portion of RAM set aside to temporarily store data. Many communication programs use a data buffer to manage incoming data during an on-line session.

230

byte. The primary unit of measurement for computer memory. As a rule, it requires one byte, either 7 or 8 bits in length, to represent each character transmitted during a modem session.

carrier detect. The process used by a modem to indicate the presence of a signal.

carrier signal. A tone generated over a telephone line that exchanges data between two computers involved in a modem connection.

communications port. Also called a COM port, this is actually a serial port installed on your PC. You must specify the COM to which your modem is attached for your communications software to work properly.

communications parameters. The "rules" two computers use to communicate with one another during a modem connection. Protocols include items such as baud rate, parity, start bits, stop bits, data rate, file-transfer methods, and the like.

communications software. Any program that allows your PC to use a modem and standard telephone line to contact a remote system.

cps. Abbreviation for characters-per-second. The number of characters transferred each second during an on-line session. Though this differs from the bps measurement, the two are related. If a computer requires 8 bits to represent each character, then the normal cps speed for an on-line session involving that PC could be approximately calculated by dividing its bps rating by 8.

CPU. Abbreviation for Central Processing Unit. The computer chip that is the brains behind your PC. Most MS-DOS computers use one of three CPU types: 8088/86 (PC/XT), 80286 (PC-AT), and 80386, all of which were designed by Intel Corporation. Recently, Intel introduced the 80486 CPU.

data word. An organized group of bits. Individual data words are organized and separated using start bits and stop bits.

default settings. The normal configuration of a piece of PC hardware or software when it is first turned on. As a rule, communications programs allow you to specify the default settings that they should use for the majority of your on-line activities.

digital signal. The types of signals generated by your PC. Generally, a digital signal is represented by either an on or off state, a 0 or 1, or some such notation. A modem converts the analog tones coming over a phone line into the digital signals required by your PC during an on-line session.

231

display adapter. The type of monitor and video board you have attached to your PC.

download. The process of transferring files and/or information from a remote system to your PC.

duplex. A communications parameter used to indicate how characters entered at the keyboard transmit to your monitor. In full-duplex mode, characters are only visible on the local monitor after they are sent to the remote system, which retransmits back over the line for display. In half-duplex mode, characters are sent directly to your monitor, without first making the journey to and from the remote system.

E-mail. Abbreviation for electronic mail. The process of transferring messages (usually ASCII text files) over a modem and telephone line.

emulation. The process of configuring your PC to resemble a specific terminal type. Many communications programs, for example, allow you to emulate a DEC VT100 terminal to enable PC-to-mainframe communications.

external modem. A stand-alone modem that is not installed inside your computer. As a rule, you connect an external modem to your PC through a serial port.

full duplex. A condition where the letters and commands you enter on-line are first sent to the remote system and then echoed back to your display monitor. (If you cannot see what you type on your monitor, change the duplex setting for your communications software to half duplex.)

half duplex. A condition where the letters and commands you enter on-line are immediately sent to the display monitor by your PC. [If everything you type during an on-line session appears twice on your monitor (e.g. yyoouu ssee tthhiiss), you need to change the duplex setting for your communications software to full duplex.]

Hangup. The command many communications programs use to transmit an + + + ATH0 sequence to your modem, resulting in it dropping the telephone connection.

Host system. A computer (either a PC or mainframe) set up to accept calls from a another system. Many PC communications programs can be set up to run in Host mode.

internal modem. A modem you install directly into an expansion slot inside your PC.

kilobyte. A unit of measurement used to specify file size. One kilobyte, or K, equals 1024 bytes.

232

local system. A relative term used to identify the system you enter commands into during an on-line session with a remote system like CompuServe, or a BBS. (See *remote system*.)

modem. The device used to convert analog tones to digital signals, and vice versa, during an on-line session. Modem is a contraction for *mod*ulate/*dem*odulate, the technical term for this process.

modulate. To change or modify some aspect of a carrier signal in a prearranged manner to transmit information over a modem connection.

off-line. The condition of being disconnected from a remote system.

on-line. The condition of being connected to a remote system.

packet-switching network. An electronic "switchboard" of sorts, used to contact a number of on-line systems. The two most popular packet-switching networks for PC communications are SprintNet and Tymnet.

parameters. See *communications parameters*.

protocol. The rules and line settings two computers use to initiate and then verify file transfers and data transmission. As a rule, PC communications programs support a number of popular file-transfer protocols.

RAM. Abbreviation for Random Access Memory. The dynamic memory on your PC used to load and execute application programs.

real-time conference. An on-line session during which several users communicate with one another over a modem link. Most commercial information services sponsor regular real-time conferences in a number of areas of special interest.

remote system. A relative term used to identify the system you are communicating with during an on-line session. (See *local system*.)

ROM. Abbreviation for Read Only Memory. Nonvolatile memory used to permanently store information in your PC. For example, your computer's initial startup procedures are stored in ROM. The contents of ROM cannot be altered by the user.

script. A series of preset sequences or activities which execute whenever that script runs. Scripts allow you to automate many on-line activities you would otherwise have to initiate manually.

search. The process of locating particular information during on-line research. Most research systems allow you to use Boolean logic to extract specific records from their databases.

233

SIG. Abbreviation for Special Interest Group. Generally, a special area within a commercial on-line service or BBS where individuals with shared interests meet. (On CompuServe, SIGS are more commonly referred to as Forums.)

start bit. An identifying bit transmitted during an asynchronous modem session. The start bit marks the beginning of a character.

stop bit. A data bit that marks the end of a character during an asynchronous modem session.

sysop. Abbreviation for SYStem OPerator. The individual responsible for maintaining a BBS, or a specific SIG area within a BBS (or on-line commercial service).

telecommunications. The process of using your PC, a modem, and a special program to communicate with another computer over standard telephone lines.

upload. The process of transferring files and/or information from your PC to a remote system.

Index

bits, 17, 230
  data bits, 22-23
    specifying during program
      installation, 59
  start bits, 233
  stop bits, 22-23, 233
BLAST, 194-195
blocks, 18, 230
bombs, 127
bps (bits-per-second), 19, 230
  versus baud, 19-20
BRB, 104
broadcast groups, 99-100
BTW, 105
buffers, 18, 230
bulletin board system, *see* BBS
BYTE Information Exchange
  (BIX), 89, 171
bytes, 17-18, 230

C

Call Waiting, 41-42, 207
Carbon Copy Plus, 199-200
carrier detect (CD), 230
  light, 73
  switch, 209
carrier signal, 230
Close-Up, 200
CMEE, 74-77, 171
  communications
    parameters, 75
  registering with, 78-84
COM port, 204-205
  see also serial ports
commands, 57
  AT, *see* AT commands
commercial on-line
  services, 168
  AT&T Mail, 174
  BBS, 176-184

BYTE Information Exchange
  (BIX), 171
CompuServe, 168-169
Computer Monthly
  Electronic Edition
  (CMEE), 171
DELPHI, 169-170
Dow Jones News/
  Retrieval, 170-171
E-mail services, 174
GEnie, 173
MCI Mail, 174
Prodigy, 172
Western Union
  EasyLink, 175
communications
  parameters, 230
    baud rate, 21-22
    parity, 23-24
  port, 230
  programs, 57
    Dialing Directory, 38
    functions, 37-38
    Installation utility, 58
    manuals, 39-41
    preparing for use, 57
    specifying default
      settings, 58-61
  software, 230
CompuServe, 74, 89-90,
  168-169
  access numbers listing,
    216-219
  BYE command, 228
  connecting to, 92-94
  Datastorm, 120-122,
    125-126
  EXIT command, 224-225
  FAX services, 136
  Forums, 221

236

237

238

241

242